FREAKY FOLKLORE

FREAKY FOLKLORE

TERRIFYING TALES OF THE WORLD'S MOST ELUSIVE MONSTERS AND ENIGMATIC CRYPTIDS

DARKNESS PREVAILS

WITH CARMAN CARRION

castle

— CONTENTS —

AFRICA

AUSTRALIA AND NEW ZEALAND

ASIA

INTRODUCTION

When I was six years old, I encountered a monster. My mother warned me that if I misbehaved, the bogeyman would come and snatch me away. One night, after a particularly exhausting day of squabbling with my younger brother, the bogeyman appeared to me in a dream. This enormous, hairy creature seized me by the ankles and dragged me beneath our house.

Luckily, I woke up.

But ever since that day I have been captivated by monsters, cryptids, and all sorts of beasts, along with the spine-chilling tales that accompany them.

These monsters all serve a purpose—or at least, they used to. Throughout history, many of them were created by concerned parents to safeguard their children from harm or dissuade them from engaging in misbehavior. Today, almost all of these legendary monsters offer entertainment to those of us who love to feel scared.

The word "monster" originates from the Latin word *monstrum*, which means "godlike premonition, unbelievable phenomenon." Hence it became the term used to describe creatures that fulfilled this role in orally transmitted stories. However, on the contrary, cryptids—creatures that have been reportedly sighted but have not been scientifically proven to exist—are not intentionally created or fabricated, yet they can fulfill a similar purpose.

In this book, we will examine the most notorious folklore monsters from six continents. You may be familiar with some of these monsters, while others may be completely unknown to you. A brief history of each creature will be followed by a short story, in *Freaky Folklore* style, about someone who may have encountered one of these monsters. The stories are not based on real people or experiences; regardless of whether you think there are monsters out there or not, I hope you'll find this book to be both fun and enlightening.

For the sake of clarity and simplicity, only a small part of the vast collection of monsters and cryptids from around the world will be included in this book. Each one of these legendary creatures is a representation of the region's culture, values, and beliefs.

AMERICAS

The Americas encompass not only the continents of North and South America, but also Central America and the Caribbean. A variety of legends flourish in these parts, reflecting a diverse blend of cultural influences to create something truly freaky.

North American folklore features tales of creatures not only from the fifty states of the United States of America, but also from Canada, the continent's many tribes of the Indigenous Peoples of North America, and Mexico. From the desolate backroads of the US Midwest to the dense forests of the Pacific Northwest, and still more to the sparkling beaches of Mexico, always be on your guard, for you never know what monsters might be around the corner.

It shouldn't come as a surprise that a region like Central and South America would abound with monster legends, with incredibly high mountains, wide waterways, and lush jungles full of rare animals. These legends are often known in more than one country, each having different names for the monsters. But whatever you happen to call them, speak softly, for saying their names might just summon these monsters to your side.

SKINWALKER

A SINISTER, SHAPESHIFTING NAVAJO LEGEND

FREAKY FACTS

LOCATION: SOUTHWESTERN LANDS OF THE MODERN-DAY UNITED STATES

FIRST SIGHTING: UNKNOWN

CLASSIFICATION: WITCH – SHAPESHIFTER – LEGEND

PERSONALITY: DECEPTIVE, MALEVOLENT, ENVIOUS, AND MANIPULATIVE

The Skinwalker is primarily an ancient Diné (more commonly known as Navajo) legend, though neighboring tribes such as the Hopi, Apache, and Pueblo all have their own ideas about what a Skinwalker might be.

Skinwalkers are believed to be witches or immoral medicine men or women who have attained the highest priestly level but have chosen to use their power to cause injury and suffering to other people. The Navajo refer to this witch as *yee naaldlooshii*, which translates to "with it, he or she goes on all fours." There are many kinds of Navajo witches, but this one is the most unpredictable and dangerous.

Outside of Navajo society, the legend of the Skinwalker is poorly understood, largely because locals are reluctant to talk about it with outsiders. Every tribe is cautious to discuss Skinwalker mythology with outsiders or to divulge it to anyone they do not trust.

According to Navajo folklore, the Skinwalker is described as completely nude, save for a wolf or coyote hide. They are referred to as a mutant form of the relevant animal by some Navajo people. Perhaps the skin is only a mask.

Skinwalkers are characterized as swift, agile, and hard to catch. Although there have been some attempts to shoot or kill one, these typically fail. Analogous to the Werewolf (see page 92), the Skinwalker is a shapeshifter who can alternate between human and animal forms, generally at night.

A Skinwalker can take on the appearance of any animal, such as a wolf, coyote, fox, bear, deer, or owl. Navajo mythology claims that Skinwalkers have the ability to read people's thoughts. They also have the capacity to produce whatever human or animal noise they want. In order to entice victims from the security of their homes, a Skinwalker may impersonate a family member or imitate a baby's cry. A Skinwalker cannot move naturally while taking on an animal shape, making them easily distinguishable from real animals by both humans and other animals. For some reason, even a skilled Skinwalker is unable to achieve the ideal animal gait or produce proportionally accurate-sized animal tracks.

Only by learning a Skinwalker's true human identity can he or she be defeated. This is possible if the Skinwalker is located and brought back to his or her home, or, in some tales, if a Skinwalker sustains an injury and the identical wound is later discovered on a human. According to legend, an individual of Navajo descent would have to proclaim, "[Name], you are a Skinwalker!"—first pronouncing the name in order to identify the person concealed behind the Skinwalker. Then, three days after, that person would either become ill or die as a result of the injustice they had done.

Although killing a Skinwalker in human form is very hard, there are techniques to defend yourself. One way to kill a Skinwalker is said to be to shoot it with a bullet coated with white ash.

While camping deep in the Chippewa National Forest, Minnesota, four young friends encounter this legend known by the Navajo. But will any of them live to tell the tale?

"I'm safe up here," Sky murmured to herself. The teenage girl sat flat against the floor of the rotting wooden watchtower. The edges of the platform beneath her were not far, and she dreaded the thought of inching closer to peer over.

Jeremy had gone out to retrieve kindling for the campfire. He never came back. They found little more than his left sneaker and a bloody human tooth.

Garret and Kaitlyn had gone to look for him. Garret had come back, struggling to describe having seen Kaitlyn getting dragged away by her scalp.

Sky had then gone with Garret, attempting to escape the forest and find their way back to the truck. Landmarks began to repeat. There was no way, Sky wondered, that this forest contained the same moss-covered wooden sign with the same writing misspelled

SPEARFINGER

A Cherokee legend that has the ability to shapeshift in order to lure her prey. Numerous accounts of her trickery include shapeshifting into her victim after hiding the body and entering the victim's home to wait until the family is asleep before taking all of their livers.

Parents would caution their children about exploring the forest by themselves because Spearfinger would be waiting for them, and made sure their children understood she would pose as their "grandmother or favorite aunt."

Skinwalker

in an identical way every hundred yards. Even so, they had indeed passed such a sign over a dozen times. When Sky broke down and fell to her knees, Garret yelled at her to get up. When she did not respond to him, he left her.

It took her a couple of hours to try to stand up on her trembling legs. By then, she could not see or hear Garret in any direction. She had become lost. Meandering off the path, hoping for a change in scenery and perhaps finally finding a way out, she stumbled upon this decrepit watchtower. Quickly, she climbed it, thinking the sooner she was up, the less likely that "thing" would see where she had gone. Surely it hadn't seen her climb up here, she thought, whatever that thing might be.

"Sky!" A familiar voice called up from somewhere below. It sounded deep, gravelly, and winded.

"G-Garret?" Sky could hardly whisper. Even with her friend nearby, she quivered at the thought of giving away her position. Clearing her throat, she tried again, keeping a wide berth from the edges, "Garret!"

"Sky? Thank God, you're okay!" The pitch of the voice heightened, and frantic footsteps followed. Garrett sounded close to the base of the watchtower.

"I–I thought you'd left me." Sky's eyes watered. Her stomach tightened.

"I'm sorry, Sky. I shouldn't have left you. I was scared." She heard a *thunk, thunk* as he began climbing the steps of the watchtower. "I am coming up."

For some reason, as the footsteps got closer, Sky's heart began to beat faster against her chest. And then finally, the footsteps stopped just before the hinged door in the floor.

Suddenly, the door flew open with such force that some of the old wood splintered and flew off, scattering around the floor. Sky should have screamed, but she couldn't. She was paralyzed with fear.

"Garret?" was all that she could manage to utter before witnessing the top of her friend's head slowly ascend from the hole in the floor. His hair was a disheveled mess, and his face was coated in a mixture of sweat and mud. Wide-eyed and with his mouth agape, Garret's appearance sent a wave of revulsion through Sky, causing her to vomit. She realized in horror that the only thing attached to Garret's head was a large hand with long, hairy, clawed fingers gripping it by the scalp.

BIGFOOT

THE WORLD-FAMOUS HIRSUTE HORROR

FREAKY FACTS

LOCATION: PACIFIC NORTHWEST

FIRST SIGHTING: LATE 1800s

CLASSIFICATION: CRYPTID –
HUMANOID

PERSONALITY: EXTREMELY SHY

Bigfoot legends predate written history and have been told
throughout the world. In North America, particularly in the
Northwest, there are legends of 8-foot-tall (2 m) hairy men
prowling the forests, occasionally frightening campers, hikers,
and hunters. Many of those who believe in Bigfoot or claim to
have seen one say they are 8-foot-tall (2 m), hair-covered bipeds
with apelike characteristics that leave proportionally
large footprints.

Although some wilderness visitors claim to have smelled their stench or heard their screams and whistles, they are typically described as non-aggressive animals that are shy and cunning, making them illusory and hence rarely observed. Despite the fact that Bigfoot is most often linked with the mountainous West of North America, the creature is known by a variety of names throughout a wide range of cultures.

The majority of Bigfoot sightings take place in the Northwest, where the beast is connected to local tribal myths and tales. According to the *Oregon Encyclopedia*, the word "Sasquatch" is a derivative of the word *sasq'ets*, which is from the Halq'eméylem language used by some Salish First Nation peoples in southwest British Columbia. Its definition is "wild man" or "hairy man."

There is little physical evidence to support the existence of Bigfoot, making it a cryptid, similar to the Chupacabra (page 63) or Loch Ness Monster. But that doesn't stop Bigfoot enthusiasts from claiming to have seen the ape that never displays its face, nor does it halt purported sightings of the creature.

In the late 1800s and early 1900s, settlers in North America began to record sightings. In 1894, a photo was taken in Canada. Then there was the discovery of footprints in 1958. Later on, a few grainy videos added to the mystery. Bigfoot sighting reports have ranged from enormous, upright apes to hairy humans, at times over 8 feet (2 m) tall and described as solidly muscular.

Research and discussion are ongoing. Groups frequently comb the Northwest woods in quest of conclusive evidence, and entire organizations have been formed to investigate, document, and verify the existence of Bigfoot.

Matt Moneymaker is a TV personality and the founder of the largest of these organizations. Five hundred people work for Moneymaker's Bigfoot Field Researchers Organization (BFRO), which was established in the middle of the 1990s and examines reports of Sasquatch sightings across North America. The largest and most established organization of its kind, the BFRO today consists of scientists, journalists, and other professionals from a variety of fields.

The BFRO's researchers are working on several investigations in both the field and the lab that deal with different facets of the Bigfoot phenomenon. The BFRO is widely regarded as the most reputable and respected investigative network engaged in the research of this topic, because of the training, experience, and caliber of its members' work.

Bigfoot

The legend of Bigfoot has become so ingrained in American culture that you can find its image on ball caps, t-shirts, and mugs. You also find this creature in movies and at theme parks created in its honor. You can even find its silhouette, cut from wood or metal, as lawn decoration in the yards of many homes. If Bigfoot could get an image copyright, it would be the richest cryptid in the world.

❖

Most Bigfoot encounters are alarming but not scary, for Bigfoot, after all, seems to be a shy creature. However, in this story, Jack and his dad, Brian, find out that even Bigfoot can have a bad day.

Under the cloak of darkness, the dense forest enveloped Jack and his dad, Brian, as they ventured toward the tree stands. The air was filled with a symphony of woodland sounds and the earthy aroma of nature. Their flashlight beams danced across the undergrowth, searching for the narrow path. The hoots of an owl could be heard softly in the distance, welcoming the night.

After half an hour of trudging through the woods, they finally arrived at their destination. Jack settled into the wooden stand, arranging his backpack and rifle. His nerves tingled with excitement and apprehension. Hunting in the dark had always unsettled him, yet he loved the thrill of the wait.

A couple of hours passed uneventfully. The woods were eerily silent, as if holding its breath. Then a bone-chilling howl rang out, echoing through the trees. Jack froze in place, his heart pounding.

"Awoooooooo."

What kind of animal made that sound?

His dad shifted uneasily beside him. "Did you hear that?" he whispered. Jack nodded, not trusting himself to speak. Brian sniffed the air and frowned. "Smells strange . . . like a skunk, but not quite."

A loud crack made them jump. Something was moving through the underbrush, heading their way. Jack gripped his rifle tightly, straining to see in the darkness. He caught a flash of movement and breathed a sigh of relief. It was just a squirrel.

But the sounds grew louder and more frequent: heavy footsteps, snapping branches, rustling leaves. It was too much noise for a squirrel. Jack's mouth went dry as the sounds came closer and closer. He glanced at his dad, whose face was taut with tension.

Were they being hunted? And if so, by what? Jack didn't know. All he knew was that they may no longer be at the top of the food chain.

A menacing growl emerged from the darkness, sending a chill down Jack's spine.

Two glowing eyes peered at them through the trees, glinting with a curious light. Jack gasped as the creature stepped into a patch of moonlight, revealing a hairy, apelike beast standing on two legs. His heart nearly stopped. They were dealing with something unnatural. Something that shouldn't exist.

Jack gripped his dad's arm, unable to tear his eyes away from the monster. "Dad," he whispered hoarsely. "We have to get out of here. Now."

Brian nodded, his eyes never leaving the creature. "Slowly," he whispered back. "We don't want to startle it."

Jack's heart thundered in his chest as he carefully reached for his backpack. He didn't want to make any sudden movements and attract the monster's attention. Sweat trickled down his forehead, his whole body tense with fear.

Suddenly, the creature let out a deafening roar, baring its sharp teeth. Jack froze, his heart in his throat. The monster charged toward them, its massive form crashing through the underbrush. Brian grabbed Jack's arm and pulled him to his feet, sprinting toward the narrow path.

The creature was gaining on them, its powerful muscles propelling it forward with terrifying speed. Jack could hear its ragged breaths and the thud of its feet hitting the ground as it crashed through the forest.

THUD, THUD, THUD!

They were never going to make it.

Jack and Brian didn't slow down until they reached the safety of their cabin. They locked the doors behind them, both panting from the sprint. Jack leaned against the wall, his mind still reeling from the encounter.

Brian's face was grim as he tried to catch his breath. "I've heard stories about creatures like that," he said, his voice low. "But I never thought I'd see Bigfoot with my own eyes."

BEAST OF BRAY ROAD

WISCONSIN'S OWN WEREWOLF

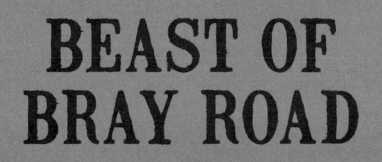

FREAKY FACTS

LOCATION: ELKHORN,
WISCONSIN, UNITED STATES

FIRST SIGHTING: 1936

CLASSIFICATION: CRYPTID –
SHAPESHIFTER – CANINE

PERSONALITY: ELUSIVE BUT
AGGRESSIVE

A bipedal creature similar to Bigfoot has been spotted numerous times since 1936 on a country back road in Elkhorn, Wisconsin. It is known as the Beast of Bray Road, named after the street where it has been most frequently seen. The creature has also been sighted more recently in Racine, Walworth, and Jefferson Counties in the 1980s and 1990s. Those who have encountered the beast claim it is engaged in activities such as eating, hunting, or scavenging.

The locals often perceive the Beast of Bray Road as a werewolf, while some cryptozoologists consider the sightings to be "another" form of Bigfoot encounters. Historical accounts suggest that the Beast may have existed since the time of Wisconsin's first settlers, who spoke of canine-like creatures that would attack before vanishing completely. Witnesses describe the Beast of Bray Road as an enormous entity, standing between 6 and 7 feet (around 2 m) tall, with a humanlike body covered in fur or hair, a head resembling that of a wolf, and large, burning, red or orange eyes.

Despite its furry appearance, witnesses report that the creature possesses a muscular physique similar to that of a man. They claim to have observed it running and walking on all fours and, at times, even on its hind legs. It has even been seen sitting on its haunches or assuming a kneeling position like a human.

In the 1980s, numerous incidents were reported where the beast allegedly made contact with cars, leaving behind extensive scratch marks on the doors and trunks. One witness recounted striking something while crossing Bray Road. A large, wolflike creature with crimson eyes is said to have followed the woman back into her car after she got out to inspect what she had hit, and left claw marks on the back passenger-side door. There have even been reports of sightings during the daytime, with several witnesses claiming to have seen an extremely large, wolflike monster crawling across cornfields on all fours. One claimed the animal they saw was chasing a deer. Whatever it is, the creature seems to have no intention of revealing itself anytime soon.

Bray Road seems eerier than most country back roads on long, dark nights, and as Julie finds out, it is the worst place in Wisconsin for your car to break down.

The long country road stretched endlessly into the night, shrouded in darkness. Bullfrogs croaking in chorus hinted of a nearby pond or lake, the only sound breaking the eerie silence.

Julie gripped the steering wheel tightly, her knuckles turning white. Panic rose in her chest as she glanced at the fuel gauge—the needle had dropped to "E." Her car sputtered and died, the engine giving one last wheezing gasp before falling silent. "Son of a . . ." she swore under her breath.

She was alone. Stranded in the middle of nowhere.

As Julie peered out the window, a shape in the ditch caught her eye.

A large dark figure was crouching on all fours, obscured by the shadows. It was eating something—the wet, tearing sounds reached her ears.

Julie froze in place, her heart pounding. What was that thing? It seemed humanlike, with bulging muscles under matted fur. But the head . . . it had a wolf's snout and jagged teeth, dripping with blood.

The creature looked up, fixing its gaze on the car. A menacing growl rumbled in its throat as it prowled toward her, advancing with an animalistic lope.

"No, this can't be real. I must be hallucinating." Julie fumbled for her phone with trembling fingers and dialed 9-1-1, choking back a sob. The dispatcher's voice grounded her as the creature circled her car, snarling.

"Stay calm. Help will come. You're not alone."

Julie repeated the words in her head like a mantra, struggling to keep the panic at bay. The creature let out a bone-chilling howl, as if sensing her fear. She gripped the phone tightly, her only lifeline in this waking nightmare.

The beast was out there, watching and waiting. Hungry for its next meal, and she was afraid that it would end up being her.

Minutes crawled by like hours. Julie huddled in the driver's seat, listening to the creature's heavy breaths outside. Its claws scraped against the metal, and she flinched at every strike.

In the distance, she could hear the faint wail of sirens. Julie nearly wept in relief as red and blue lights flashed through the trees, illuminating the road.

The sheriff's patrol car pulled up behind hers, and an officer stepped out. "Miss, are you all right?" His gaze shifted to the hulking figure beside her car, hackles raised in a menacing stance.

The sheriff drew his gun in one smooth motion. "Freeze! Put your hands up and get on the ground, now!"

The creature let out a roar, lips peeling back to reveal dagger-like teeth. It crouched, ready to pounce—

A gunshot split the air. The creature shrieked in pain, clutching its arm. In that moment of distraction, the sheriff fired again.

The beast howled and fled into the night, melting into the shadows of the forest. An uneasy silence fell over the road.

The sheriff rushed over to
Julie's car, pistol still at the ready.
"Did that thing hurt you, Miss?"
His eyes were grim, haunted.
No doubt he had also seen what
she had in those brief glimpses
under the headlights.

Julie shook her head, pulse
racing. "No, I—I'm all right." She
peered at the dark woods where the
creature had disappeared, a chill
running down her spine.

It was out there, and there
were now two more witnesses to
the existence of the Beast of
Bray Road.

Beast of Bray Road

GOATMAN

HALF GOAT, HALF MAN, ALL MYSTERY

FREAKY FACTS

LOCATION: MARYLAND, UNITED STATES

FIRST SIGHTING: 1957

CLASSIFICATION: CRYPTID – HYBRID

PERSONALITY: AGGRESSIVE, MYSTERIOUS, MENACING, AND ELUSIVE

The frightening tales of a creature that is half man, half goat have long haunted the state of Maryland in the USA, but sightings of this creature have also been reported in Louisiana and Texas.

According to Maryland residents, the Goatman is mainly found in the city of Bowie. This humanlike, hairy creature is said to carry an axe, which it uses to kill both animals and humans. Numerous people claim to have encountered this vicious creature.

There are myriad myths and stories surrounding the Goatman that Marylanders firmly believe in. However, the legend of the Goatman remains shrouded in uncertainty, turning this century-old case into an unsolved mystery.

Accounts of the Goatman vary, but most descriptions portray it as a humanoid with a face and a body that surpass human characteristics, one that is covered in hair. Other depictions liken the Goatman to the fauns of Greek mythology, in that it has a human upper body and the lower body of a goat.

Some say the creature stands between 4 and 12 feet (1 and 4 m) tall, though most sightings place the Goatman at around 6 to 8 feet (around 2 m) in height. When provoked, the Goatman emits a high-pitched squealing sound.

Stories have been told that claim the Goatman makes its home somewhere in the forested northwest region of Prince George's County, close to Bowie, living in a makeshift shelter. The Goatman is sometimes said to kill stray dogs or randomly attack cars with an axe.

One variation of the legend's origin suggests that a genetic scientist at the Beltsville Agricultural Research Center was conducting experiments involving animal DNA. In one such experiment, the scientist introduced a goat into the laboratory to test his theories.

Regrettably, the scientist took an ill-calculated risk by sequencing and injecting a human gene into the goat's DNA, resulting in disastrous consequences. A ferocious creature with a humanlike appearance was born, posing a potential threat to mankind.

The goat-man creature subsequently fled from the laboratory, seeking refuge in the woods of Maryland. As local residents began to witness the creature, it gained notoriety and became known as the "Goatman." Although there have been many sightings of the Goatman reported from the forests of Maryland, no one has yet been able to prove its existence.

Many people have claimed to have seen the Goatman in the forests of Maryland, but not many have come as close as the fourteen-year-old girl who came face to face with the creature in October 1986.

Stephy's heart raced with excitement as she climbed onto the hay-filled wagon for the Fall Festival hayride in rural Maryland. The air was crisp, carrying the scent of fallen leaves and damp earth. As the wagon creaked to life, she stole a glance at the boy she had recently met at church, Justin. His presence as her date for the evening brought both comfort and excitement to the eerie setting of the night.

The wagon ventured off the familiar main road, onto a secluded path flanked by dense woods. The moon created a ghostly glow, casting elongated shadows that danced like phantoms on the forest floor. Stephy clung to her friends, laughing nervously, as they approached a dark, old country road that seemed to lead into the heart of the woods.

It was then that Stephy noticed something unsettling. The hayride had veered from its usual path, and she exchanged uneasy glances with her friends. But before they could voice their concerns, the wagon jolted to a stop, stuck in the mud.

The atmosphere grew tense as the wagon's young occupants waited for the adults to come up with a solution. The woods seemed to close in around them.

From the west side of the forest came a haunting sound—the eerie bleating of a goat.

Baa, baa, baa!

It was like nothing she had ever heard before. She glanced at Justin, who looked equally unnerved.

Then, as if in response, the bleating began to surround them. *Baa, baa, baa*! It moved from one side of the woods to the other, encircling the wagon. Panic began to set in, and the children huddled together for safety.

Suddenly, rocks began to pelt the wagon, as if thrown by invisible hands. *Thwack. THWACK*! The onslaught was relentless, and the terrified children covered their heads, trying to shield themselves from the unexplained assault.

Stephy's heart pounded in her chest, and she dared to peek through her fingers. Her eyes widened in horror as she saw the woods come alive with movement. Shadows flitted between the trees, and she caught glimpses of a dark figure with glowing eyes and elongated limbs. The creature had horns, fur, and hooves like a goat, but it looked disturbingly like a man as well.

"It's the Goatman!" someone shrieked, and the name sent a chill through the air. The legend of the Goatman had circulated around the small town for years, but Stephy had always thought it was just a scary story.

As the children's screams echoed through the woods, the wagon suddenly lurched forward, breaking free from the mud. The nightmare wasn't over yet. Stephy watched in horror as the jerking force of the wagon breaking loose from the mud sent one of the kids

Goatman

flying over the side of the wagon. "Justin!" she screamed as she watched the horse-drawn wagon leave him in the middle of the muddy road.

They were going so fast, and the noise of the turning wagon wheels and drumming hoofbeats of the horses was so loud that it took several minutes to get the adults to understand what had just happened. She had been the only one to witness Justin's fall. By the time they had stopped, turned the wagon around, and went back, Justin was gone.

They searched the woods for an hour but found no sign of him. The kids were taken back to the church, and the sheriff's office brought out a search team. They scoured the area for several days, but the only thing they ever found were hoofprints in the mud on the old, dark country road.

WENDIGO

CANNIBALISTIC NIGHTMARE OF THE NORTH

FREAKY FACTS

LOCATION: NORTHERN UNITED STATES AND CANADA

FIRST SIGHTING: SEVENTEENTH CENTURY

CLASSIFICATION: EVIL SPIRIT – SHAPESHIFTER

PERSONALITY: COLD, INHUMAN, CANNIBALISTIC, DESPERATE, AND MALEVOLENT

According to Ojibwe, Saulteaux, Cree, Naskapi, Innu, and Algonquian folklore, the Wendigo is a mythical beast or malevolent spirit that is said to prowl the woodlands along the coast of the United States and Canada, especially in the Great Lakes region.

It is thought to be a representation of the dangers of pride as well as the winter spirit. Though opinions differ, the Wendigo is typically seen as a terrifying monster with a ravenous appetite for human flesh. Anyone who comes into contact with a Wendigo runs the risk of being eaten or possibly transformed into one themselves.

Although the Wendigo was initially depicted in early Algonquian folklore as a demonic type of being, or an evil spirit without any physical form, over time the supernatural being came to be thought of as a beast. According to Ojibwe beliefs, Wendigos are enormous creatures with slim bodies.

The creature's most notable trait is an insatiable appetite for human flesh, which explains why they appear so slender but also so large. According to legend, no matter how much human flesh they ingest, Wendigos are never satisfied and full. With each feed they tend to grow larger.

According to the Algonquian legend, the terrifying creature has pale, ashy skin that is tightly stretched over its protruding bones like a latex suit. Its glassy eyes reflect the moon from their sunken, dark sockets, appearing blank yet brooding with evil.

As the beast chases its prey from a looming height of 15 feet (5 m) in the pitch-blackness of the forest, a terrible stench emanates from its skin, thick with decay and newly spilled metallic blood. Those who claim to have seen the monster in the flesh seem doomed by this horrifying vision.

Some versions of the legend say that the Wendigo has the ability to imitate human voices, which it uses to lure prey.

According to a part of the relevant legend, a stag's skull is set atop its shoulders, adorned with sharp fangs and a large tongue—which are two of its other standout characteristics.

The monster appears as a byproduct of cannibalism and dark magic in the infamous North American folktale. It is believed that if a man or woman eats human flesh, they will become a Wendigo. One may also turn into a Wendigo as a kind of retribution for immoral or forbidden behavior. According to certain myths, merely meeting a Wendigo might cause someone to turn into one. They could even dream of being possessed by the beast. The beast then takes on the identity of the individual after seizing control of its victim.

Wendigos are outstanding hunters because they are incredibly strong, resistant to harsh weather, and possess keen senses. When injured, they have the ability to regenerate and mend their bodies.

According to certain beliefs, the Wendigo would slowly drive its prey insane before attempting to lure them away with a repulsive odor that only it can detect.

In the book of Proverbs of the Hebrew Bible there is a verse that says, "Pride cometh before a fall." Many men and women have found that proverb to be all too true. Grant finds out just how hard one can fall, and, when you do, let's hope there isn't a Wendigo waiting to spread the icing on the fallen cake.

Grant, a successful businessman, had planned a trip to the Rockies alone for much-needed time to think after his wife had left him and taken their son with her. He knew it was his fault for neglecting them in favor of his business and his friends. He thought the cold mountain air would clear his head and help him figure out how to get his family back.

He arrived early in the morning, just as the first snow of the season began to fall, and hiked for a few hours before pitching his tent. Thoughts of his wife and son filled his mind as he set to work. Little did Grant know that the minute he had entered the forest something more sinister than his own personal demons was stalking him.

WECHUGE

The Wechuge is a giant cannibalistic creature from Northwestern Canada, similar to the Wendigo.

The Athabaskan people of Northwestern Canada told stories about this cannibalistic monster. According to legend, a Wechuge is a human who has been overcome by the spirit of a large animal and turned into a gigantic beast as a result.

Wendigo

As he lay in the tent that night, trying to fall asleep, he heard the rustling of leaves. "It's just a deer," he told himself under his breath as he listened.

Then he heard a twig snap.

Then another.

Grant sat up, his heart beginning to race, and listened intently. The crickets were no longer chirping; the night had grown silent.

A pungent odor drifted through the tent fabric and began to burn his nostrils. It smelled of rot and decay, causing Grant to fight back the urge to gag. He had covered his nose and mouth to fight the stench at about the same time he heard a soft voice.

"Hello? . . . Is anyone in there? It's cold out here, and I am so hungry."

It sounded like a young girl, but Grant didn't understand why a young girl would be out in the forest alone late at night. Something was very wrong here; Grant could feel it deep in his bones. The voice was coming from something evil. He slowly reached into his bag and quietly pulled out the revolver he had brought for purposes other than protection.

He listened as whoever or whatever was out there snorted and began slowly pacing around the tent. Tinkling laughter began to fill the air and turned into a deeper, more horrid, demonic sound as it reached the opening that was still zipped tight. Suddenly, the laughter stopped, and the bright moonlight cast a silhouette over the top of the tent.

Grant could clearly make out a massive rack of antlers atop broad shoulders. The figure looked enormous, but before Grant could even raise the gun, the tent began to rip as razor-like claws tore into it. A gaping hole appeared in the top of the tent, and Grant found himself staring into the empty sockets of an antlered skull. The creature had pieces of rotted flesh hanging in strips from its towering body.

It looked down at Grant and leaned forward, causing a large, slimy, black tongue to droop from its mouth. Grant knew that he was looking at a kindred spirit, a being of gluttony and greed, and the face of his death.

JERSEY DEVIL

CURSED BEAST OF THE PINES

FREAKY FACTS

LOCATION: PINE BARRENS OF
SOUTHERN NEW JERSEY,
UNITED STATES

FIRST SIGHTING: 1812

CLASSIFICATION: CRYPTID –
FLYING BIPED

PERSONALITY: NOCTURNAL,
ELUSIVE, MENACING, AND
MALEVOLENT

More than 265 years ago, a winged monstrosity of legend was born in the form of the Jersey Devil. Since the early 1700s, it has terrified, perplexed, and intrigued the people of New Jersey.

The story officially begins when Mrs. Leeds of Smithville became pregnant in 1735. Mrs. Leeds felt older than her years because this would be her thirteenth child.

As her labor began one stormy night, she yelled out during a fit of terrible contractions: "Let this child be a devil!" When the midwife handed Mrs. Leeds a beautiful baby boy, she quickly forgot her painful labor. However, the baby's body suddenly started to change, and Mrs. Leeds watched in terror as the child's face lengthened to resemble a horse or bat, with long, dark wings that emerged between his shoulder blades.

Mrs. Leeds had spoken the Jersey Devil right into existence, as her words had been a curse upon the newborn.

The Jersey Devil has a horrendous appearance with a wide array of physical traits, making it one of the most intriguing cryptids.

During its transformation, the horns on the top of its head were the first to appear. Next were its razor-sharp claws that emerged at the end of its arms, followed by black fur and feathers that covered most of its body. It grew at an alarming rate and didn't stop until it reached somewhere between 6 and 10 feet (2 and 3 m) in length.

Lastly, it grew a forked tail and two bat-like wings. Its eyes began to glow a fiery red, completing its transformation. The monster's scream, which sounded like a tormented human being as well as a vengeful predator, was the saddest and most horrifying thing to hear.

Many of the friends who had assembled in the chamber, including the midwife, were slaughtered by the beast. According to some reports, everyone was killed besides the child's parents. Afterward, it flew up the chimney and into the woods, where it still dwells today.

The Jersey Devil is one of the less well-known cryptids thought to live in North America, but its story may be the spookiest. It's a terrifying creature that lives in the New Jersey Pine Barrens, an eerie forest where few people have the courage to go too far.

It has reportedly killed livestock, other animals, and, according to some accounts, even people throughout the years. It has driven workmen away from the forests, propelled others to the brink of insanity, and rendered law enforcement personnel helpless. The Devil, however, has never been apprehended, despite tens of thousands of sightings dating back almost three centuries.

In our modern world of handheld instant entertainment, one person can reach millions in just a matter of seconds. Will recognized the potential that this advanced communication had as he watched young gamers just like him becoming hugely successful, and he wanted in on it. But success would come at a high price.

Shooting off his mouth had kept Will in constant trouble growing up, but on his YouTube channel it worked to his advantage most of the time. That was until one brilliant idea led him to the most terrifying encounter of his life.

Will wanted to grow his fan base because he needed more subscribers if he wanted to make the big bucks. With the help of two of his best friends, Brad and Dennis, they came up with an idea they thought would work.

He changed his channel name from *Will Thrill* to *Will or Will Not*. He then recorded a video and told his fans to dare him to do crazy things. Brad and Dennis would choose one dare each week, and Will would either accept the dare or be offered an alternative that was equally distasteful or terrifying.

Now, Will had only lived in Chatsworth, New Jersey, for the past year, but he had heard the Jersey Devil stories and, quite frankly, they freaked him out. So, when a subscriber, with the username "BadDevil," dared him to spend a night in the Pine Barrens, he wanted to refuse the dare.

But he couldn't. This was just what his channel needed. Brad and Dennis were very supportive, of course, and promised to be with him every step of the way. This was a relief to Will; he was afraid he could never do this alone.

A week later, Will found himself deep in the Wharton State Forest with his ragtag film crew. Even though they planned to fake the whole thing, Will was constantly on edge. He didn't believe in monsters, but the idea of them petrified him.

That night, they were sitting around the fire discussing their plans when the forest around them fell silent. "Hey, has it been this quiet all night, or am I just spooking myself?" Will asked Brad.

"Dude, I don't think so, but I wasn't really paying attention until just now." Brad seemed genuinely nervous. Dennis had been tending to the campfire, and just as he settled back into his spot across from Will, the silence around them was shattered by the sound of timbers crashing in the forest.

The boys sat upright, their eyes like saucers.

"You guys better not be trying to scare me," Will warned in a hoarse whisper.

Neither Brad nor Dennis replied. They were busy looking around the campsite at the tree line.

Another crash came from the opposite side of the camp, closer than the one before. This brought the boys to their feet. They didn't even realize that they had huddled in with their backs to each other, each facing a different area of the forest.

Brad cursed in pain as the fire licked his leg. He had gotten too close without even realizing it. When he jumped, Will and Dennis jumped too, taking their focus away from the forest, until a screech that vibrated their eardrums sent them into total panic mode.

The three large, teenage boys ran to the tent, almost tumbling over one another trying to get in. Regardless of a lot of cursing and shoving, they were finally all inside. Will was sure that if he hadn't been so scared he would have laughed, because they must have looked much like the Three Stooges.

After securing the tent's opening, they lay there for what seemed like ages, not speaking. The night was quiet except for their heavy breathing.

Will was starting to calm down and was about to speak when a flapping sound again broke the silence. The boys froze and listened as it grew closer.

The tent began to shake. Will thought he heard Dennis whimpering. The flapping grew closer and suddenly there was a tearing sound from above. A huge opening appeared as the top of the tent began to gape open.

Then the quiet engulfed them again. The tent went still, and slowly they began to breathe. They were a tangle of limbs, hugging each other so tight it was hard to tell where one boy began and the other ended.

The quiet was slowly replaced by the sound of the breeze shaking the rip in the tent, and it was gradually joined by the sound of crickets.

Sometime later, probably exhausted from fear, the boys fell asleep.

The sun filtering into Will's eyes stirred him from his sleep. He pried Dennis's arms from around his back and shoved him aside. Brad was already awake but just lying there, staring at the large tear that had once been the roof of their tent.

Waking Dennis, they cautiously exited the tent and searched the area as they gathered their things to leave. Everything was scattered all around, but nothing was missing.

The boys went home. They watched the video they had made and began to edit, but to their surprise, something amazing had happened.

Jersey Devil

That night, when they dove into the tent, someone must have kicked the camera because it had come on and they had got some good footage of a large, winged creature shredding their tent. The Jersey Devil episode went viral.

AMERICAS
—

MOTHMAN

CRIMSON-EYED CRYPTID AND HARBINGER OF DOOM

FREAKY FACTS

LOCATION: WEST VIRGINIA, UNITED STATES

FIRST SIGHTING: 1960s

CLASSIFICATION: CRYPTID – HARBINGER OF DOOM

PERSONALITY: MYSTERIOUS, DISTURBING, OMINOUS, AND ELUSIVE

Five men were digging a grave on November 12, 1966, in a cemetery close to Clendenin, West Virginia, when they observed a humanoid shape soaring low from the trees directly over their heads.

Two young couples fled the surrounding woods later that month in the little town of Point Pleasant, West Virginia, claiming to have encountered a terrifying creature. They told the sheriff about what happened and said that other than its 10-foot (3 m) wings and brilliant red eyes, the thing resembled a human in most ways.

The "Mothman" was featured in the local newspaper. The population as a whole gathered in the area where the creature was reported in a matter of days, armed and prepared to hunt it down. Despite not finding it, they managed to start a legend.

There has never been a sufficient description of the Mothman's feet or face. One witness who could clearly make out the face could only describe the details as horrifying and terrible. Afterward, she experienced horrific dreams and came dangerously close to losing her mind. These were the first sightings of the creature that came to be known as the Mothman. Other accounts describe the Mothman as a winged humanoid figure resembling something part human and part moth. It is said to stand roughly 8 feet (2 m) tall and is brownish to black in color, with glowing red eyes.

Anyone who gets a good glimpse of the Mothman tends to experience severe anxiety and mental anguish, which can often linger for months or years. People claim that when they look into the Mothman's eyes, they are filled with a sense of absolute evil.

The victims of what appears to be the Mothman's favorite pastime—chasing cars—have revealed that he can fly much faster than any bird should be able to. He will occasionally soar in front of them and strike the roof.

There were numerous reports of sightings from all across Point Pleasant, then these gradually expanded. Eventually, there were reports of the Mothman both abroad and in other parts of the United States.

However, sightings in Point Pleasant ended following a tragedy. A year after the first sighting in 1967, the Silver Bridge, a crucial entrance and exit from the town, collapsed, killing over forty people. In the aftermath, individuals reported seeing the Mothman standing on the bridge the day before, perhaps as a sign of impending doom.

There has been plenty of folklore born from superstitious minds, and even if you aren't superstitious, strange happenings combined with tragedy may change your mind. It only takes one encounter to make most people a believer.

In 1900, Galveston was a booming metropolis in Texas, with a population of 37,000, rivaling New York City. Jean Williams worked there for the Galveston Railway Company;

he took the job after marrying his young wife, Maggie, who at the time was expecting their first child, Tom. Jean, now in charge of freight handling, was short-handed one evening when something strange happened.

While sorting through crates in a train car, Jean noticed what looked like someone crouching behind a large crate. Cautiously, he approached the figure and saw two bright orbs that resembled eyes. The orbs emitted a shining red light. Before Jean could react, the figure spread arms like wings and crashed through the gangway door, disappearing into the night.

Startled, Jean jumped backward and tripped over the freight, injuring himself and causing several crates to fall on top of him. With Jean unable to work due to broken ribs, young Tom took on the role of providing for the family. Meanwhile, Jean began experiencing terrifying nightmares about the birdman he'd seen, waking Tom with his screams every night.

Tom asked his father about the nightmares, and what he told him was unsettling. Ever since he had seen the birdman, he would dream of the same thing every night: The large bird would be sitting on the fence in front of the house, looking at him through a window. When he would go outside to shoo it away, he could hear screaming and roaring in the distance. He would look out toward the ocean and see a giant wave. Every time he tried to rush his family to safety, the wave would swallow them up. Tom's father said that the dream was so vivid that he could feel the water filling his lungs and the panic in his chest.

Worried about his father's mental state, Tom kept his concerns to himself until one dark night after work. As Tom attempted to unlatch the gate to their home, he heard a whistling sound. Assuming it was the wind, he proceeded to latch the gate when he heard rustling from the roof. Looking up, Tom saw a figure that resembled a man but had large glowing eyes like an insect.

Frozen in place, Tom locked eyes with the creature. The mesmerizing moment was shattered when the creature stood tall, spread its enormous wings, and vanished into the night like a shooting star. That night, Tom had the worst nightmare of his life, with his father by his side. He dreamed that the ocean swallowed the island of Galveston, along with their home. In his dream was that same red-eyed creature that he had seen outside. It was now Tom's turn to wake up screaming.

He couldn't help but wonder if the dream was some sort of premonition. Was the creature—half man, half bird or moth, or whatever—trying to tell them something? An overwhelming sense of foreboding hung over him until, finally, the dream was revealed.

Mothman

On Saturday, September 8, 1900, a week after Jean Williams first saw the creature with red eyes in the train car, the Great Galveston Hurricane came ashore. The storm caught the Williams family, along with most of the population of Galveston, by surprise. Tom and his youngest brother were the only surviving members of their family. The hurricane claimed between 6,000 and 12,000 lives, with no confirmed death count.

MICHIGAN DOGMAN

A CANINE LEGEND WITH A HUMAN HOWL

FREAKY FACTS

LOCATION: MICHIGAN, UNITED STATES

FIRST SIGHTING: 1887

CLASSIFICATION: CRYPTID – CANINE

PERSONALITY: NOCTURNAL, ELUSIVE, AND FRIGHTENING

There are plenty of scary and disturbing tales to be found throughout the Great Lakes State, but one legend in Michigan stands out. Whether or not you believe in the supernatural, the tale of the Michigan Dogman may convince you to keep an eye out when you go on future getaways.

According to legend, the Dogman is a 7-foot-tall (2 m) canine/human hybrid. He is reported to have a dog's head on a human torso, with eyes that are either bright blue or amber. As if the Dogman's appearance alone weren't frightening enough, according to legend, he also makes a frightful cry similar to a person screaming.

The Lower Peninsula's northwest is where the majority of sightings have taken place. Confirmed sightings of this terrifying creature go all the way back to 1887, so it is nothing new. It's believed that two lumberjacks traveling through Wexford County were the first to spot the Dogman. They claimed to have witnessed a creature that they said had a dog's head and a man's body.

In 1937, Robert Fortney was assaulted in Paris, Michigan, by five wild dogs. He claimed that one of them walked on two legs. In the 1950s, Allegan County received reports of similar creatures, and in 1976, Manistee and Cross Village did as well.

Steve Cook, a disc jockey at WTCM-FM in Traverse City, Michigan, recorded the song "The Legend" in 1987. He first played it on April 1 as a practical joke. He based the song on accounts of the beast from long ago. Cook gave Bob Farley, a music producer and songwriter, credit when he recorded the song with a keyboard accompaniment. After finishing the song, Cook started receiving phone calls from listeners who claimed to have run into a similar creature.

Even if skeptics have dismissed the sightings as a hoax, Michigan residents will defend the legend fiercely.

Some people go hunting for cryptids, hoping for an encounter that they can document, possibly bringing proof to the world that the legends are true. But most people encounter them accidentally and, many times, unwillingly.

It was late spring in Augusta, Michigan. The chill had left the air, and hikers and campers were already beginning to enjoy the change of the season. Sadie was staring out the window of her English II classroom, thinking about her plans for her last summer before starting college. She was also planning on how to break up with her high-school boyfriend, Derrick. They would be going their separate ways soon, and besides, he had become more ill-tempered over the last year.

There was an end-of-the-year bonfire party planned out by the lake near the Fort Custer Recreation Area. Everyone would be there. She would talk to Derrick after the party, if she could even get him to go.

She did manage to convince him, but not without a fight, and on the way there, the argument continued. The whole evening was miserable; Derrick was rude and hateful to everyone. Sadie finally demanded that he take her home.

They left the same way they came, but somewhere along the route they took a wrong turn. Still in the midst of a heated argument, neither of them noticed their mistake until the car rammed into something large and dark standing in the road.

Derrick slammed on the brakes.

"What the hell was that?" Sadie asked.

"I don't know," he barked back. "Maybe a dog or something. Let me go look and see if it messed up my car."

Sadie followed him out of the car and replied snidely, "Maybe you should make sure it isn't injured as well."

They walked around to the back of the car. "Oh, God!" Sadie heard him say, before she saw what he was looking at. She leaned around him to see what it was.

They watched in disbelief and shock as the doglike creature rose onto all fours. It was probably a foot (30 cm) taller than either of them. Sadie was about to speak, but Derrick shushed her. That's when she noticed the look on his face. It was such an obvious look of terror that it was instantly contagious.

Simultaneously, they bolted back to the car, jumped in, and slammed the doors shut.

"Sadie, where's your cell phone? Call for help." Derrick begged.

She began quickly digging through her pockets, but her hands came out empty. "I—I must've dropped it on the ground," she said, "when I jumped into the car."

She covered her ears trying to block out the sounds of snarling. "Where's yours?"

"I left mine at home." Derrick began to yell. "You idiot, can't you ever do anything right!"

The car was shaking, Derrick was yelling, and Sadie was crying.

Sadie tried to burrow down into the small floorboard space to put as much distance between her and this beast as possible. She waited for the window to shatter, but to her relief it didn't.

Michigan Dogman

Derrick had been watching in horror until the moment when fear overcame him. He panicked and jumped from the driver's side of the car, taking off to run through the woods, leaving Sadie abandoned and alone.

The Dogman—as that was most likely what it was—seized this moment by leaping on top of the car, causing a loud thud, and then jumping off. It headed into the woods in pursuit of Derrick, its prey.

Sadie, still huddled up in a ball on the floorboard, began to sob. Her eyes were closed and at first she was too scared to open them, but as she heard the growls growing more distant, she finally did.

She had to make a decision. Should she try to run, or close the door and remain safely inside the locked car? But was she really safe inside the car? Too scared to run, Sadie quickly leaned over, grabbed the door handle, and slammed the door shut.

A few minutes later, while still hiding in the floor of the car, she nearly jumped out of her skin when something landed on the roof of the car with a loud thud.

She tried to burrow herself deeper into the floorboard as she quietly listened.

Sadie was staring up at the driver's side window when something fell from the roof of the car and dangled there. For a moment she hoped she was seeing things.

It looked like an arm.

She didn't dare crawl out of her hiding place to get a better look. She just stared at it until it started to move. The fingers began to open and close, but just as they did another loud thud sounded on the roof of the car, followed by screams of agony and terror.

The screams weren't the only noise she heard, either; they were accompanied by the sounds of snarling and the ripping of flesh. Blood began to trickle down the glass of the window.

Shortly after, the night went silent again, but only for a moment.

Sadie jumped when she heard the creature climbing off of the car. She covered her mouth and nose with her hand, afraid that it would hear her breathing.

She heard it circle the car, sniffing at every inch as it passed. When it reached her side of the car, it stopped.

A low, rumbling growl began just on the other side of the door closest to where her head lay.

She began to cry, no longer needing to hide. It knew she was there.

The sound of her crying caused the beast to begin clawing at the door. It sounded like it was trying to dig its way through.

She knew that it was just a matter of time before it tore its way into the car, and she would soon share Derrick's fate.

WAHEELA

THE GREAT WHITE WOLF OF THE CANADIAN AND ALASKAN TUNDRA

FREAKY FACTS

LOCATION: NORTHERN REGIONS OF CANADA AND ALASKA

FIRST SIGHTING: LATE NINETEENTH CENTURY

CLASSIFICATION: CRYPTID – CANINE

PERSONALITY: FEROCIOUS, ELUSIVE, MYSTERIOUS, AND AGGRESSIVE

Inuit folklore has preserved the story of this prehistoric bear-dog beast. The Waheela is a cryptid that resembles a wolf and is reportedly indigenous to Alaska and Canada's Northwest Territories. However, it may move southward during the winter. As a result, claims of seeing Waheela-like creatures have allegedly been made as far south as Hearst, Ontario, and northern Michigan.

Compared to wolves, the Waheela is more robust. Folklore holds that the Waheela resembles the Arctic wolf (*Canis lupus arctos*) in appearance, although it is much taller, heavier, and more robust than other wolves. According to some reports, the Waheela stands between 3½ and 4 feet (1 m) tall at the withers, with an average height of approximately 3½ feet (1 m).

Like the Arctic wolf, the Waheela has thick white fur. However, according to other accounts, the Waheela resembles the Northwestern wolf (*Canis lupus occidentalis*), a gray wolf subspecies also called the Mackenzie Valley wolf, whose coat could be black, white, gray, brown, or bluish in color. Furthermore, witnesses have reported that the Waheela has splayed toes and tracks that measure around 8 inches (20 cm) in width.

Although wolves hunt in packs, the Waheela is thought to be a lone hunter. According to certain Inuit legends, the beast is unharmed by weapons, making it unstoppable. The Waheela is powerful enough to kill a bear, although it prefers simple food like young, elderly, or injured animals. It might go after a victim that was nursing and seize its offspring. The beast is also said to attack any and all people it encounters.

Three trappers were allegedly cruelly torn to pieces by a Waheela in northern Michigan. The legend goes on to tell that when the Waheela encountered campers, it would promptly *chomp* off their heads in one rapid motion. Thanks to the Waheela's actions, the Nahanni National Park in Canada gets the moniker "Headless Valley."

Even the Kushtaka (page 52) is not as scary as a creature that looks like a cross between a polar bear and a wolf. It makes you wonder what a run in with one of these creatures would be like. Are they vicious creatures by nature or just misunderstood?

There are countless hunting stories told and retold by hunters, but the most chilling ones are about the hunter becoming the hunted. Sometimes nature likes to turn the tables, especially when a legendary creature is involved.

In the rugged mountains of British Columbia, there was a problem with overpopulation of timber wolves. There were so many of them that they began to kill cattle and sheep. The people living in the area were afraid for their own safety.

Tom McAllister, a rugged middle-aged man with a scruffy beard and piercing blue eyes, eagerly accepted the challenge of culling the overpopulation of timber wolves in the infamous Nahanni Valley, also known as the Headless Valley.

Tom's rucksack was packed with all the essentials—tent, sleeping bag, knife, matches, and enough rations for a week. His blue eyes shone with excitement as he set off down the winding trail. The forest loomed before him, dark and dense. The smell of pine filled the air as he ventured deeper into the wilderness.

The wolves' distant howls reverberated across the valley as Tom pursued them throughout the days and into the nights. Their footprints were visible all over the snow-covered ground, serving as a continual reminder of their presence. Tom was an accomplished hunter, though, and the excitement of the chase kept him going.

One evening, right around sunset, Tom set up camp near a small stream. The crackling fire provided warmth against the biting cold. The night was still, except for the occasional hooting of an owl and the distant howls of the wolves.

As Tom lay in his sleeping bag, the sounds of the forest seemed to grow louder, closer. A strange scent filled the air, a mix of wet fur and damp earth. Tom's instincts told him something was amiss, but he shrugged off the unease, attributing it to his nerves.

The next morning, Tom continued his hunt. He followed a fresh trail of wolf prints, leading him deeper into the valley. The terrain became rugged and treacherous, but he pressed on with determination. Hours passed, and he found himself in a dense thicket, the canopy overhead blocking out most of the daylight.

Suddenly, a low growl reverberated through the air. Tom froze, his heart pounding in his chest. The sound was unlike anything he had ever heard before, causing the hairs on the back of his neck to stand on end. He gripped his knife tightly, ready to defend himself.

More growls joined the chorus, and the air was thick with tension. Tom's blue eyes darted around, trying to catch a glimpse of the source of the growls. But all he could see were shadows dancing between the trees.

In the distance, the howls of timber wolves rose in a haunting symphony. The noise seemed to close in on Tom, surrounding him on all sides. He could feel the presence of something massive and sinister lurking in the darkness.

When it stepped out of the tree line, Tom's breath caught in his throat. It was massive! It was a wolf, but it was easily larger than a grizzly bear. Fear clawed at his chest as Tom realized what he was looking at. He had heard the legends since he was a kid but he had never really believed them. But here it was looking down at him from its towering height. The Waheela.

"Easy there, big fella. Let's not do anything we'll regret." Tom tried to soothe the beast.

With a deafening roar, it lunged at Tom, teeth bared and claws outstretched. As the Waheela lunged at him, time seemed to slow down. He could see every detail of the beast's massive form, its fur matted and stained with the blood of its previous kills. Its eyes, like pools of golden fire, bore into his soul, and its snarling maw revealed rows of razor-sharp teeth.

Tom's heart raced, and he raised his knife in a desperate attempt to defend himself. But the Waheela was too quick, knocking the weapon from his grasp with a powerful swipe of its paw. Tom stumbled backward, his mind racing for a way to escape.

The beast circled him, growling menacingly, its hot breath steaming in the frigid air. Tom's senses were overwhelmed by the stench of wet fur and the earthy scent of the forest. He could hear the crunch of snow beneath the creature's massive paws and the echoing howls of the timber wolves in the distance.

With a surge of adrenaline, Tom lunged at the Waheela, trying to use his own strength to overpower the beast. But the creature was relentless, dodging his attacks with uncanny agility. Its claws sliced through the air, leaving deep gouges in the trees around them.

Each attempt to fight back only seemed to anger the Waheela further. It let out another bone-chilling roar, shaking the very ground beneath them. Tom's chest heaved with exhaustion, and he knew he couldn't keep this up for long.

In a last desperate bid for survival, Tom sprinted toward a nearby rock formation, hoping to climb to higher ground and gain an advantage. But the Waheela was faster, and before he could reach safety, it pounced, knocking him to the ground with brutal force.

Pain shot through Tom's body as the beast's claws tore into his flesh. He screamed in agony, but the sound was drowned out by the Waheela's triumphant snarls. With a

Waheela

final swipe of its massive paw, the beast delivered a fatal blow, and darkness enveloped Tom's vision.

The valley was silent once more, save for the triumphant howls of the timber wolves. The Waheela stood over its fallen prey, its eyes glinting with malevolence. It had claimed another victim, and the legend of the deadly beast would live on.

AMERICAS

KUSHTAKA

ALASKA'S COASTAL CRYPTID

FREAKY FACTS

LOCATION: ALASKA AND CANADA
(ESPECIALLY BRITISH COLUMBIA)

FIRST SIGHTING: 1900

CLASSIFICATION: CRYPTID –
SHAPESHIFTER

PERSONALITY: MISCHIEVOUS,
DECEPTIVE, MYSTERIOUS, AND
(IN SOME CASES) PROTECTIVE

The Tlingit peoples of what is now known as the Pacific
Northwest tell tales of shapeshifters that await people who
explore the wild or the sea. These creatures are known as
Kushtaka. The Kushtaka is a mythical shapeshifting creature
capable of assuming human or otter-like form, and potentially
other forms too.

They share the same nature and appearance as the Skinwalkers from the Central Plains, depending on the tribe's legend. Some have been reported as demon-like, while others are closer to an otter-like yeti. That could be the reason why they are also known as Alaska's second Bigfoot.

When someone is hurt or in danger, these Kushtaka sometimes appear, and at first glance they seem to be humans.

They will promise to assist or save anyone they come across, but legend has it that the Kushtaka take their prey farther into the wilderness and transform them into their own kind.

Some versions of the legend claim that these malicious beings lure sailors to their deaths, while others attest that they rescue children who have become lost in the bitter cold, only to turn them into Kushtakas as well.

Numerous legends describe the Kushtaka as having a high-pitched, three-part whistle that goes low-high-low. Others claim that the Kushtaka lure their prey with the sounds of a newborn or a distressed woman, or entice women to rivers by imitating the cries of newborns before deciding whether to kill and tear them to pieces or transform them into more Kushtakas.

Locals hold that only four things—copper, urine, dogs, and fire—can fend off these cunning critters. Additionally, the locals always travel to the water in pairs and keep their kids away from the water in a safe manner.

There are many dangers in the Alaskan wilderness, and some people have been unfortunate enough to meet those dangers when they appear disguised as cute, furry animals.

Mel had grown up in Ketchikan, Alaska, but had moved away to explore the world once she was grown. As many stories go, she met the love of her life in another country, fell in love, and settled down far from Ketchikan. When tragedy struck and she lost her love years later, she returned home to heal.

The flight to Ketchikan seemed to take forever, but thankfully, the drive afterward was a short one. Within an hour of landing, she was in a rental car, bumping down the short dirt lane to her childhood home. It was almost dark and Mel was lost in thought, reliving memories of her youth when something large darted out in front of the car. She hit the brakes and scanned the road, but whatever it was had vanished into the trees. As she put the car into drive, she thought she saw a pair of glowing yellow eyes watching her from the dark of the forest. It reminded her of the otters that played in the creek behind the house, but it was way too big to be an otter.

She shrugged it off, figuring it to be a deer or something larger, and headed on down the road. Her brother's car was in the driveway, indicating that he was home. Bruce met her on the porch when he heard her car pull up, and she remembered she hadn't told him she was coming.

"I know we discussed it, but I didn't think you would really come, and without warning. The house is a mess. I could've picked you up at the airport," he said, as he stepped off the porch and gave her a big hug.

"I know, but I wanted to surprise you, and I don't care if the house is a mess," she said over his shoulder as he was squeezing the breath out of her.

Bruce had to work, so she had the house to herself for the next few days. She looked at pictures and spent a lot of time reminiscing, but eventually, her favorite place began to call to her—Ketchikan Creek.

She threw on a jacket and some boots and headed down the path behind the house. There was a light dusting of snow on the ground, and as she walked, more snowflakes began to fall. Nostalgia washed over her as she felt like she was stepping back in time.

She could hear the icy water lapping over the rocks as it rolled by, and she could hear the otters playing even before she saw them. As the creek came into view, she saw that there were two of them. She watched for a while, enjoying their shenanigans the same way she had when she was a kid. She watched until they eventually wandered off back into the forest.

Mel turned and headed back toward the house. She hadn't gone far when she heard a chittering sound from behind her. She turned around to discover that the larger of the two otters was following her.

He stopped when he saw that he had been spotted and stood on his hind legs, chirping. Mel smiled before she spoke to the little furry creature, "Why are you following me? I don't have any fish." She took a step toward him, and he dropped down on all four feet and began growling.

She shook her head, giggled at the creature's rude behavior, and began to walk away. She could hear his tiny steps behind her as they made little crunching sounds in the snow.

Kushtaka

She was beginning to feel uneasy. Otter attacks were rare but not unheard of; they usually had to be provoked, but all she had done was laugh at the little guy. Mel began to walk faster, hoping to lose him.

It was weird because it sounded like the otter's footsteps were getting heavier with every step she took. She finally stopped again and glanced back.

Instantly, she wished she hadn't. Standing there, upright, was a man that looked very much like an otter, but wasn't.

LA LLORONA

THE GHOSTLY RIVERSIDE WAILING WOMAN

FREAKY FACTS

LOCATION: MEXICO AND THE SOUTHWESTERN UNITED STATES

FIRST SIGHTING: NINETEENTH CENTURY

CLASSIFICATION: GHOST

PERSONALITY: SAD, ANGRY, AND VENGEFUL

Since the time of the conquistadores, the La Llorona or Weeping Woman legend has been a part of Latin American culture. According to the stories, the tall, slim spirit possesses long, flowing black hair and natural beauty. She wanders the creeks and rivers in a white gown, wailing into the night and looking for children to drag, screaming, to their watery graves.

The origins of the La Llorona legend are unknown, as well as when it began. Despite the fact that the tales differ from one source to the next, they always revolve around the same basic idea: She is the ghost of a mother who spends all of eternity searching for her lost children in rivers and lakes.

The story goes that La Llorona was a kind, loving woman named Maria, who married a rich man. This man showered her with gifts and attention. However, after she gave birth to his two sons, he changed, and he returned to his old ways of infidelity and drunkenness, often abandoning her for months at a time. He even discussed leaving the lovely Maria to marry a member of his own affluent class because he no longer cared for her.

When he returned home, it was just to see his sons, and Maria, feeling heartbroken, began to despise him. One evening, Maria and her young sons were walking along a shaded path close to the river when a carriage carrying her husband and a beautiful woman went by. He stopped, spoke to his children, ignored Maria, then drove the carriage down the road without looking back.

When Maria saw this, she flew into a terrible rage, turned on her sons, grabbed them, and flung them into the river. As they were being carried downstream, she became aware of what she had done and hurried down the bank to try to save them, but it was too late. Maria crumbled in overwhelming anguish as she rushed up and down the streets, sobbing and screaming.

Maria mourned her children day and night. She refused to eat during this time and wandered along the river in her white gown, looking for her boys in the hopes that they would come back to her. She roamed the riverbanks, crying nonstop, her gown dirty and ripped. She became thinner as a result of her refusal to eat, until she looked like a walking skeleton. She eventually died on the riverbanks while still a young woman.

Soon after she passed away, her restless ghost started to appear, wandering the Santa Fe River's banks at night. People started to be terrified to venture outside after dark because of her weeping and wailing. They began to use the tale of La Llorona as a warning for children not to get too close to the riverbank, telling them that the phantom would drag them into the water if they did.

*A parent would do anything to keep
their child safe, even facing
down a demonic vengeful spirit who
wants to steal them.*

Sophia and Carlos lived on a ranch in Arizona nearby the Santa Maria River with their two sons, Anthony and Angel. On late afternoons, they would often take their boys down to the river to relax and play before nightfall.

One day in late August, Sophia and the boys went for their usual outing by the river. When they arrived, Sophia threw a quilt down on the grassy riverbed, took off her sandals, and told the boys not to go far.

Sophia laid her head on the blanket and enjoyed the last rays of the sun as it was beginning to lower in the western sky. She slowly drifted off to sleep.

She wasn't asleep for long before she was awoken by a scream. Sophia swiftly made it to her feet just in time to catch Anthony as he flung his arms around her waist. He was yelling, "Mama, she's got Angel!"

It felt like her heart stopped mid-beat in her chest as she frantically scanned the riverbank for any sign of her youngest son. Suddenly, she heard a splash and the desperate, water-choked attempt at screams coming from the direction she had last seen them playing.

Feet still bare, Sophia ran toward the screams. Reaching the edge of the river, she caught sight of Angel's tiny head sinking into the dark waters. Sophia quickly jumped into the water and reached Angel just in time to grab his tiny hands that were still flailing above him.

As she pulled, she was suddenly met with resistance as some other force seemed to be fighting to pull him down.

Sophia quickly submerged herself enough to wrap one arm around his small waist. But as her face was just about to touch the water, she saw another face, the glowing profile of a woman with dark eyes, staring angrily back at her.

Sophia had no time to think; she had to just react. She felt her grip begin to slip. But suddenly, as she refused to let go of her son, he burst free from the water with a loud splashing sound.

She ran as best she could with her soaked child in her arms to put distance between them and whatever she had just seen in the water. She didn't take the time to check on him until she got him back to the bank, and once there she only hesitated long enough to make sure he was breathing before she hugged him to her chest and ran to grab Anthony by the hand. She left the blanket and her sandals and did not stop running until they were in the safety of their home.

Falling to her knees, Sophia hugged her sons close and cried.

PATASOLA

Another creature that started out as a bad mother is the Patasola from Colombian folklore.

She is the soul of an unfaithful woman who roams the mountains, valleys, and plains, grieving her mistake that dishonored her children and husband.

Patasola is an evil, dangerous vampire and an enemy of men who is filled with hate and spreads terror. The Patasola is feared by farmers, hunters, miners, and loggers. She hunts and seduces unfaithful husbands, using her supernatural powers to change her appearance.

PISHTACO

THE FLESH-HARVESTING BUTCHER OF THE ANDES

FREAKY FACTS

LOCATION: ANDES REGION, SOUTH AMERICA

FIRST SIGHTING: FIFTEENTH CENTURY

CLASSIFICATION: BOGEYMAN

PERSONALITY: RUTHLESS, GREEDY, PREDATORY, SINISTER, AND DECEPTIVE

The legendary Pishtaco is said to be a vampiric gringo who haunts the Peruvian Andes, earning him the notorious nickname of the "fat-stealing ghoul."

The Pishtaco is often portrayed as a foreigner with pale skin, donning high boots, a leather jacket, and a wide-brimmed felt hat. To immobilize unsuspecting travelers on midnight mountain routes and paths, he stealthily infiltrates graveyards, grinding human skeletons into powder. Then, using a large knife, he beheads and dismembers his victims in his quest to extract their fat.

According to accounts, the Pishtaco prowls the night roads. He can be seen riding a horse or, in modern times, driving a car. Some claim that the Pishtaco adopts a priest-like appearance as he casually walks along the roadside, ready to launch his vicious attacks on lone travelers, using his long knife to dismember them for their flesh and fat.

The fat stolen by this sinister entity is believed to serve various purposes. It may either be consumed by the Pishtaco or used in the creation of cosmetics, oils for machinery, and medicines. Additionally, there are beliefs that the fat is utilized in the production of holy oil used in Catholic baptisms, as well as in the maintenance of church lamps and the lubrication of bells.

Despite its comical name, the Pishtaco, a vampiric creature, is far from amusing. Its name derives from the Quechua word pishtay, *which means "to behead, slit the throat, or slice into pieces." Pishtacos lure their victims into the depths of the jungle, where they mercilessly suck out and feast upon their body fat.*

One day, a group of hikers decided to embark on a journey through the majestic Andes Mountains. Despite being cautioned about the Pishtaco, they dismissed the warnings as nothing more than folklore. Fueled by confidence and skepticism, they ventured deeper into the mountains, ignorant of the looming danger that awaited them.

As they trekked onward, an unsettling unease descended upon the hikers. They couldn't shake the feeling of being watched, unseen eyes tracing their every move. Suppressing their instincts, they pressed forward, convinced that the fat-sucking ghoul was a mere figment of the imagination.

Nightfall draped its dark veil over the mountains, and the hikers gathered around a crackling campfire, their laughter and jovial banter filling the air. Little did they know that lurking in the shadows, the hungry Pishtaco patiently watched, biding its time for the perfect moment to strike.

In an instant, one of the hikers vanished, leaving behind no trace. Shock and fear rippled through the group, shattering their carefree cheeriness. They had to face the

Pishtaco

grim reality that the Pishtaco may not have been just a story.

Desperation seized them as they frantically searched for their missing companion, but their efforts yielded no answers. The only trace of their friend was a bloody trail leading into the forest. Panic surged through their veins, forcing them to acknowledge the need for immediate escape.

With trembling hands, they hastily gathered their belongings, propelled by an urgent instinct to flee. Yet, their fate had already been sealed. Relentlessly, the Pishtaco closed in, swiftly and mercilessly, determined to claim each hiker as his prey.

One by one, they succumbed to the insatiable hunger of the ravenous creature as the Pishtaco dragged them off into the darkness, kicking and screaming. Their cries for mercy echoed in the abyss of the night, unanswered and futile. The Pishtaco reveled in his gruesome triumph, leaving behind only remnants of terror.

Only one man managed to escape, having hidden beneath the corpse of one of his companions. Covered in blood, he remained motionless, and the Pishtaco, deceived into believing he was already dead, eventually wandered back to his lair in the forest.

The sole survivor, haunted by the horrors he had witnessed, eventually stumbled back to civilization, his spirit forever marred by the horrifying ordeal. He shared his chilling tale, imploring others to believe and understand, only to be met with skeptical disbelief once more.

And so the cycle continued, with a new generation of hikers dismissing the warnings, firm in their irrational belief in invincibility. The legend of the Pishtaco lived on, guarded by the silent mountains, patiently awaiting the arrival of the next unfortunate souls who dared to test their fate against the merciless prowler of the Andes.

CHUPACABRA

A FANGED CANID CRYPTID WITH A THIRST FOR BLOOD

FREAKY FACTS

LOCATION: LATIN AMERICA AND THE SOUTHWESTERN UNITED STATES

FIRST SIGHTING: 1990s

CLASSIFICATION: VAMPIRIC CANINE

PERSONALITY: MYSTERIOUS, PREDATORY, NOCTURNAL, AND ELUSIVE

The Chupacabra is a legendary beast that has purportedly been prowling the American Southwest and draining the blood of livestock for decades. It is described as being the size of a small bear, sometimes sporting a tail, usually with scaly skin, and having a row of spines running down its back. It has long been a central figure in Mexican, Puerto Rican, and Southwest American folklore.

The Spanish name Chupacabra, which means "goat-sucker," was given to the creature because of the first animals that were allegedly killed and had their veins drained in 1995, in Puerto Rico. After that, it is claimed that the violent beast turned its attention to lambs, chickens, rabbits, cats, and dogs.

People did not know why hundreds of farm animals were dying bloodlessly. When the news of the slaughtered farm animals spread, farmers in other countries began speaking up about assaults on their own livestock. Animals were apparently being killed in similar ways in Mexico, Argentina, Chile, Colombia, and the United States.

The origin theories for Chupacabras are as diverse as the sightings themselves. Many people believe it came from top-secret government genetic research conducted in Puerto Rico's rainforests. Some say that it is an extraterrestrial being that was transported to Earth by a spaceship. Others claim that the strange monster is part of some evil biological warfare scheme, or perhaps the manifestation of divine wrath.

Strange and elusive cryptids have appeared all around the globe, but none as strange as the blood-sucking Chupacabra. The stories of this creature are sure to be passed down for many generations to come, just as in this next story.

Miguel's grandfather had told him the story so many times that he could retell it as if he had been there himself. Out of all of his grandpa's stories, this was the one that scared him the most.

Since the 1970s, Miguel's grandfather and his family had lived in Mazunte, Oaxaca. It was a small village in Mexico, nestled between a wide beach that was thought to be one of Mexico's most beautiful, and the Sierra Madre del Sur mountain range. It was in that small village where he was raised on a little farm, and it was on that farmland that he saw it.

He claimed that he had gotten up early one morning to do his chores so that he could rush into town to meet a girl who had recently moved there. He fed the cow and chickens first, then the four goats last because they were always so noisy. His grandfather said he expected them to greet him with their usual loud bleats, but instead he was met with silence.

As he reached for the gate, he noticed that it was only supported by one hinge and had claw marks running from top to bottom. He stepped over the gate and into the pen, immediately concerned. The goats weren't in their usual spot, so he looked around with the kerosene lantern he was carrying.

He noticed the first one in an unusual position, lying on its back with its feet up. He took a closer look, thinking it was sleeping, only to discover that its throat had been ripped open. He searched the rest of the pen and discovered the second goat huddled in a corner, shaking and terrified. The third he discovered dangling from the top of the enclosure, as if it had attempted to escape, but its neck had also been ripped open.

Miguel's grandfather said he knew he'd have to wake the others if he wanted to find the fourth goat before it was killed like the other two. He, his father, and his two younger brothers, who were eight and twelve years old at the time, searched the entire area well after sunrise but found no trace of the missing goat. They buried the other two goats and locked the remaining one in the barn.

Chupacabra

His grandfather was tasked with repairing the broken gate while his father finished the chores. He could hear his younger brother Gabriel playing in the yard. He was about to nail a piece of wood to the bottom of the broken gate when he heard Gabriel scream. He jumped up and ran in the direction of the house, where Gabriel's screams could be heard. He froze for a split second at the sight before him.

Gabriel was lying on the ground near the yard's edge, with an animal twice the size of a goat on his back. Except for the pointed spines running down its back, this creature resembled a hairless, leathery-skinned dog. It had Gabriel by the back of his neck and was viciously shaking its head as Gabriel tried to crawl away. The sound of gunfire jolted him, and he saw the creature drop his brother and flee. He might have lost his brother to that mysterious creature if it hadn't been for his father's quick action. Miguel's grandfather would never forget seeing what he believed was a Chupacabra.

EL SOMBRERÓN

GUATEMALA'S GHOSTLY SERENADER

FREAKY FACTS

LOCATION: GUATEMALA

FIRST SIGHTING: FIFTEENTH CENTURY

CLASSIFICATION: HUMANOID SUPERNATURAL BEING

PERSONALITY: MISCHIEVOUS, AMOROUS, EERIE, AND TRICKY

You can find a bogeyman legend in every culture, but in Guatemala, he wears a sombrero. Although he may go by several names, such as Tzizimite, Tzipitio, and the goblin, El Sombrerón frequently takes the form of a short man clad entirely in black. He also pops up in other Latin American nations, such as Mexico.

El Sombrerón wears shiny black boots that click as he walks and a glittering black belt. He sports an enormous black sombrero on his head.

He frequently has a horse, whose mane and tail are braided. His favorite thing to do is court attractive young women with large, dark eyes and long, black hair, which he enjoys braiding for her. He will sing to her and play his guitar, but he might also put dirt on her plate and cause her to have trouble eating and sleeping.

El Sombrerón typically shows up near dusk, and at times he will be driving a group of four mules through the city. He will then tie the animals in front of a girl's house and start serenading her with songs and playing music with his sparkling silver guitar when she seems to favor his advances. El Sombrerón will sometimes dance with her too.

Young ladies are warned by the story of El Sombrerón to be respectful of tradition, family values, and social norms, because males with evil intentions may try to entice them using the moonlight and music. They may risk falling prey to a mysterious stranger's attractions on a moonlit night if they fail to do this.

There are so many bogeymen in folklore, but few that only target young girls. Like many children, though, these girls don't always listen to cautionary tales and warnings, and that usually leads to a bad ending.

Adriana was angry with her parents for taking her away from her home and her friends in Colombia to live in Guatemala, where she knew no one. It was all she could think about, to the point that she struggled to make new friends.

The days at a school full of strange faces were lonely, but the nights when she was alone with her thoughts, longing for her old room, her old friends, and her old life that now seemed so far away, were the loneliest.

One night, Adriana couldn't sleep, so she stepped out onto her balcony to gaze up at the stars. The crickets were chirping a melancholy tune, and the scent of jasmine wafted through the air.

Suddenly, the crickets grew silent, and their tune was replaced with another. It was the soft sound of a guitar playing a sad song. She knew that music, yet she couldn't place it.

As the final notes faded, a figure emerged from the shadows, and Adriana knew immediately who was making the music. Every Latino child had heard the legend of El Sombrerón.

LA DIABLESSE

Half woman, half demon, this creature also preys on the opposite sex. La Diablesse, often described as a stunning devil woman, stalks her male victims while wearing long, lovely gowns and a huge straw hat that conceals her face.

She appears on nights when the full moon is the only source of light, waiting in dark and lonely places where a man might pass and deviate from his path to accommodate her lovely face. Her one cloven hoof is concealed by her long clothing. Frequently emerging from behind trees, she casts spells on her unsuspecting male victims, luring them into the woods.

These males are unable to catch up with her and eventually become disoriented and lost. Confused and frightened, the victims try to find their way home but often meet a horrific fate in the process.

A man dressed all in black with a wide-brimmed hat and a mischievous grin stood in her garden, staring up at her balcony, his fingers poised over the frets of his guitar.

Adriana opened her mouth to scream, but no sound emerged. She stood frozen to the spot, trapped by the gaze of the dark figure who had stepped out of her childhood nightmares into reality.

Adriana gripped the balcony railing, her knuckles turning white. She tried to look away from El Sombrerón's piercing gaze, but she couldn't tear her eyes away. His fingers plucked a single note on the guitar, and a wave of peace washed over her, calming her frayed nerves.

"There's no need to be afraid," El Sombrerón said, his voice as hypnotic as his music. "I've come to take away your loneliness, your heartache, and your longing for a home that is no more."

Adriana wanted nothing more than to flee, but her body remained motionless. "What do you want from me?" she whispered.

"Simply to give you a gift. A chance to forget." El Sombrerón's fingers danced across the frets, playing a few bars of a cheerful tune from her childhood in Colombia.

El Sombrerón

Tears sprang to Adriana's eyes as memories flooded back. She could smell the roses by her old bedroom window and hear her friends laughing at some silly joke.

"I can give you more," El Sombrerón said softly. "I can make this feeling last forever. All I ask for in return is your devotion."

Adriana gripped the railing tighter, struggling to surface from the waking dream. She had to get away, had to warn someone about the danger lurking in the garden. But the music held her in its thrall, tempting her with the promise of blissful oblivion.

"What do you say?" El Sombrerón asked, his grin widening. "Will you be mine?"

Adriana opened her mouth, unsure of the answer that might emerge. Was forgetting worth the cost of her soul?

She teetered on the edge of a precipice, ready to tumble into an abyss of no return, and found that she no longer cared.

DUENDE

MISCHIEVOUS KNEE-HIGH TRICKSTER

FREAKY FACTS

LOCATION: EL SALVADOR, SPAIN, AND PORTUGAL

FIRST SIGHTING: UNKNOWN

CLASSIFICATION: HUMANOID

PERSONALITY: MISCHIEVOUS, CAPRICIOUS, PROTECTIVE, AND PLAYFUL

In El Salvador, a small dwarf creature called El Duende may be an evil entity or a protector, depending on who is telling the story.

Duendes are believed to be somewhat shorter than 2 feet (1 m) tall, but don't let their small stature deceive you—when they want to, they still have plenty of punch. Duendes come in both genders, and both have a fairly similar appearance. They have long hair that covers them, and in some cases they wear no garments. The males may have beards.

According to folklore, this elf-like creature either dwells in the forest or within the walls of children's bedrooms. When the opportunity arises, it has been said that the Duende will either lead children to his cave in the middle of the forest or emerge from the cave's walls to crudely clip a child's toenails, sometimes even removing the entire toe!

Duendes, like most fairy creatures, can be good or bad depending on the situation or the person. They are very protective of their homes and the boundaries they have created to live in. Even if you unintentionally threaten a Duende's home, you could be tormented mercilessly.

According to some legends, a Duende can only be seen by children, but if you drink just enough alcohol to get a little drunk, you might catch a glimpse of one out of the corner of your eye.

Duendes are especially fond of children. If a child becomes scared or lost, their parents encourage them to call out to the Duendes for guidance.

In a quiet village nestled on the outskirts of the forest, children shivered beneath their covers, terrified of a visit from El Duende when the sun would set.

El Duende wasn't always considered an evil creature.

Legend had it that El Duende was a cheeky being, a small creature with a long, gray beard and a mischievous twinkle in his eyes. The villagers believed that encountering him would bring bad luck and misfortune. However, there were those who questioned this notion and wondered if El Duende could be more than just a bringer of darkness.

One day, a young girl named Maria ventured into the forest. Her parents warned her of the dangers that lurked there, but Maria, curious and adventurous, brushed off their concerns. She had a sparkle in her eye, an indomitable spirit that refused to succumb to fear.

As Maria wandered through the enchanting woods, the sunlight filtering through the leaves created a dappled dance upon the forest floor. She hummed a joyful tune, her voice carrying through the gentle breeze. Suddenly, movement in the bushes caught her attention. Maria's heart raced as she approached the source of the commotion.

And there, amidst the verdant foliage, stood El Duende. She recognized him immediately. His small stature and peculiar appearance were exactly as the stories had described. Yet, in that moment, Maria sensed something different about him. The mischievous glint in his eyes held a touch of kindness, and his wrinkled face seemed to carry the weight of ancient wisdom.

Without hesitation, Maria offered El Duende a warm smile, a gesture of friendship and acceptance. To her surprise, El Duende returned the smile. In that instant, a connection formed, bridging the gap between their worlds. They communicated through laughter and play, their days filled with shared adventures and unbridled joy.

News of Maria's newfound companionship soon spread throughout the village. The once fearful whispers transformed into curious murmurs. The villagers marveled at Maria's radiant happiness, their skepticism slowly replaced by a flicker of hope. Perhaps, they thought, El Duende was not solely a harbinger of darkness, but a catalyst for unexpected bonds and joy.

Days turned into weeks, and weeks turned into months. Maria's bond with El Duende grew stronger with each passing day. She found solace and understanding in their shared moments, while El Duende relished the warmth of her companionship. Time seemed to slip away unnoticed, and Maria's daily excursions into the forest lengthened as their relationship deepened.

Yet, amidst the euphoria of their friendship, something crucial was overlooked. El Duende, in his playful nature, had forgotten the basic needs of a human companion. Days and nights blurred together as they danced through the forest, and hunger and fatigue silently took hold of Maria.

Tragically, one fateful day, Maria's energy waned, her body weakened by hunger and thirst. She collapsed within the depths of the forest, her frail form succumbing to the cruel grip of starvation. El Duende, caught in the throes of his own sorrow and guilt, realized too late the consequences of their blissful ignorance.

The villagers, devastated by Maria's loss, cast their blame upon El Duende. Anger and grief swirled within their hearts, painting the once-beloved creature as a malevolent force. They mourned the loss of their beloved Maria, cursing El Duende as an evil entity preying upon innocent souls.

Heartbroken and burdened by remorse, El Duende retreated into the shadows of the forest, forever haunted by the memory of the girl he cherished. As time went by his guilt

Duende

and self-loathing brought extreme loneliness, and his heart began to twist until the little Duende hated everyone, but not near as much as he hated himself.

The village clung to their newfound conviction that El Duende was a forerunner of tragedy, warning future generations of the dangers lurking within the forest. The memory of Maria and El Duende's friendship remained forever in the hearts of those who dared to remember, a bittersweet reminder that even in the darkest of places, love and innocence could thrive, if only for a fleeting moment.

EL CULEBRÓN

A HAIRY, SLITHERING GUARDIAN OF TREASURES

FREAKY FACTS

LOCATION: CHILE

FIRST SIGHTING: UNKNOWN

CLASSIFICATION: REPTILIAN –
SHAPESHIFTER

PERSONALITY: MYSTERIOUS,
CUNNING, AND PREDATORY

Known to lurk in the forests and dark caves of Chile, El Culebrón
is described as a creature resembling a large snake, with a thick and
elongated body measuring over 6½ feet (2 m) long. It is a mysterious
and terrifying entity.

 Unlike other reptiles, this legendary creature possesses a unique
feature—it is covered in hair. It has a black, fine coat, sometimes
resembling feathers. Its large head with red eyes is reminiscent of a
calf's head. While its natural form is undoubtedly frightening, it is
said to possess the ability to shapeshift into the form that will evoke
the greatest fear in its victims.

According to the legend, this large, hairy snake can primarily be found in the countryside, especially at night, although there have been sightings during the day as well. It has been rumored to attack hikers, mule drivers, or anyone unfortunate enough to cross its path. If you ever venture into the Chilean countryside, it is advised to steer clear of its known habitats.

El Culebrón is also associated with hidden treasures. It is said to appear at the locations where treasures have recently been buried. According to folklore, this creature is drawn to riches, and there is a belief that capturing it will bring about great wealth for the captor, should they possess the courage to try.

Children should listen to their parents, but more often than not, they don't. They perceive their parents as overprotective and believe that their parents simply want to spoil their fun. However, in some unfortunate instances, these disobedient children learn the harsh lesson that they should have heeded their parents' advice, as their parents were only trying to keep them safe.

The sun was setting over the Chilean countryside as Isabella made her way home from a friend's house. Her mother had warned her not to stay out too late, but she had lost track of time. While Isabella had heard the stories of El Culebrón, like most children, she never believed them. She dismissed them as tales concocted to scare young ones.

As she walked down the dirt road, she heard rustling in the bushes. She stopped and looked around but saw nothing. Pressing on, the rustling persisted, growing more unsettling with each step.

Suddenly, a loud hissing sound pierced the air from behind her. Isabella whirled around to face an enormous hairy snake, its head resembling that of a calf, fixated on her. She tried to flee, but the serpent was swift. It soon caught up to her, wrapping its massive body around her.

Isabella's desperate screams for help went unanswered as the snake constricted her with increasing force, stealing her breath. She felt her fate closing in.

PEUCHEN

This creature has three things in common with El Culebrón. It originates from Chile; it is a shapeshifter; and it is another serpent.

The most widely accepted form of the Peuchen was thought to be a winged serpent that whistled as it flew through the air. Its stare had the power to make its prey, usually sheep or other livestock, helpless, so that its blood could be sucked dry at the Peuchen's leisure.

There has also been speculation that the Peuchen myth may have been some of the basic inspiration for the contemporary Chupacabra legend (page 63) before it diversified over time and spread through other cultures.

"Please don't kill me," she begged, and to her surprise, El Culebrón seemed to listen.

"What can you give me if I spare your life?" the vile serpent hissed.

"I–I have a golden ring, but it's at home," Isabella exclaimed desperately.

Unexpectedly, the snake released its grip, slithering away into the undergrowth. Gasping for air, Isabella remained on the ground, alone and shaken.

She hurriedly made her way back home, her legs trembling with fear. Upon arrival, she discovered that no one was there. She collapsed onto her bed after locking all the doors and windows, the encounter weighing heavily on her. Isabella knew that telling her mother about her terrifying experience would only result in her disbelief and punishment for staying out too late. As she sat in silence, an eerie hissing sound reached her ears from outside the window. Rising cautiously, she peered outside, finding nothing in sight.

As Isabella turned from the window, she found herself staring into the red glowing eyes of El Culebrón.

"The ring, child, where is it?" he demanded in a long hiss.

Offering the ring had been an attempted distraction, for Isabella had lost the ring a long time ago. El Culebrón knew he had been deceived when he saw the fear in her eyes.

Suddenly, a chilling sensation coiled around Isabella's leg. When she realized the snake had been wrapping itself around her tightly, ensnaring her limb, her eyes widened in horror. El Culebrón had come to strike the death blow for her act of deception. She fought desperately to free herself, but the serpent's strength was too great to overcome. It kept tightening its hold, crushing her leg until the bones broke.

No one came to Isabella's aid despite the night being ravaged by her agonized screams. The snake persisted in its ruthless attack until her leg was reduced to a bloody stump. Slithering away into the darkness, the snake left Isabella sprawled on the floor, broken and bleeding.

Later, when Isabella's mother returned home, she discovered her lifeless daughter lying on the floor.

From that day forward, rumors spread, claiming that El Culebrón had claimed Isabella's spirit, taking her away to be his eternal bride, forever lost to the world.

El Culebrón

EUROPE

Many of the oldest folklore stories have roots in continental Europe. The British Isles, in particular, possess a rich history that predates the invention of writing. Within these lands, a plethora of beliefs and legends have been recorded, encompassing tales of witches and werewolves, the existence of fairies, and the renowned story of the Loch Ness Monster. Numerous legendary creatures that we are familiar with today are recurring figures in diverse European folktales.

BANSHEE

IRELAND'S SCREAM QUEEN

FREAKY FACTS

LOCATION: IRELAND

FIRST SIGHTING: OLD GAELIC LEGENDS (DATE UNKNOWN)

CLASSIFICATION: SPIRIT – HARBINGER OF DEATH

PERSONALITY: FOREBODING, MOURNFUL, EERIE, AND PROTECTIVE

If you were to catch sight of her, you would find yourself fervently praying for the safety of your family, as it would be highly likely that one of them would soon join her in the afterlife. She is known as the Banshee, a fairy woman and a spirit connected to the realm of the dead. The term Banshee originates from the Old Irish word *bean sidhe*, meaning "woman of the fairy mound." Her name is intertwined with the numerous tumuli, or earthen mounds, scattered across the Irish countryside. These tumuli were traditionally constructed over one or more graves and were believed to house the spirits of the departed.

The moniker "Little Washerwoman" emerged from accounts of the Banshee being spotted cleansing the bloodstains from the garments of individuals who were destined to die.

Even if you didn't actually see her, the Banshee could announce her presence through cries, weeping, or mournful keening. Legend has it that her wails possessed the power to shatter glass.

Her appearance is often described as that of a hideous old hag with blood-red eyes. Her long, gray hair is matted, and her teeth are green. She has long, bony fingers and yellow fingernails. However, in some versions, she is depicted as more enchanting, appearing as a beautiful young woman.

In the earliest accounts of Irish history, Banshees were not perceived as terrifying entities like they are today. Instead, they served as harbingers, forewarning families of the impending death of a loved one so that preparations could be made.

Furthermore, the impending demise need not have been a particularly gruesome one. It could simply be the passing of someone who had lived a long life and succumbed to natural causes. The Banshee would act as their escort, ensuring their safe passage to the other side.

However, as years passed and stories were passed down from generation to generation, the lore surrounding Banshees gradually transformed.

Today, Banshees are believed to be malevolent spirits emitting high-pitched screams. These screams are said to be so potent that anyone within earshot may experience burst eardrums and become marked for death.

Some hold the belief that only the intended victim can hear the Banshee's screams, and they will be driven to madness until they ultimately take their own life. The agonizing screams that torment them lead to self-inflicted head injuries.

There is also a belief that once the victim has perished, the Banshees will feast on the frontal lobe of their brain utilizing her long tongue, specifically designed for this gruesome purpose.

To hear the wailing of the Banshee is an instant, inescapable curse. The only thing you can do is pray and hope that your prayer is answered.

Aislinn lived a peaceful life in a small Irish village near Dublin. During the day she worked at a local dairy farm, and in the evening she earned extra cash at a small pub in town. She was content with her life and never suspected that anything could go wrong.

Late one evening, in the depths of the mist-shrouded Irish countryside, Aislinn found herself venturing into the heart of darkness. She had never believed in the tales of ghosts and demons that she had heard since her childhood, but tonight that would change.

As she left the dairy and headed to the village, the sun's last rays were fading from the sky. The air grew heavy with foreboding and dense with fog as an eerie silence blanketed the landscape. Suddenly, a piercing shriek sliced through the stillness, rattling Aislinn's bones.

Covering her ears, Aislinn craned her neck to find the source of the chilling sound. Through the mist, a figure began to emerge, clad in flowing, white garments, its face obscured by a veil of darkness.

As it approached, Aislinn stammered, "What do you want from me?" Her voice was laced with fear.

The Banshee's wail intensified, its high-pitched screams reverberating through the air. It locked eyes with Aislinn, and she felt a cold grip tighten around her heart.

"Your time has come!" the Banshee hissed. "You have been marked for death."

Aislinn's mind spun with disbelief, but as the Banshee's screams persisted, her eardrums felt as if they would burst, and blood began to trickle from them, staining her cheeks crimson. She fell to her knees, her ears ringing. She thought she would surely die right then and there, but sudden silence filled the night. The Banshee was gone.

The nights following became pure torment as the memory of the Banshee's screams filled Aislinn's mind, pushing her to the brink of madness. Sleep eluded her, and her days were filled with unbearable agony. Driven to desperation, Aislinn's hands instinctively rose to her head, nails digging into her scalp. She had to find a way to make it stop, but only one solution came to mind, over and over: eternal silence.

Banshee

MYLING

AN UNEARTHLY ENTITY, SPAWNED FROM ABANDONED CHILDREN

FREAKY FACTS

LOCATION: NORWAY, SWEDEN, ICELAND, AND FINLAND

FIRST SIGHTING: OLD NORSE LEGENDS (DATE UNKNOWN)

CLASSIFICATION: VENGEFUL SPIRIT

PERSONALITY: RESTLESS, SORROWFUL, SEEKING, AND VINDICTIVE

In Scandinavian folklore, the Myling is considered one of the most disturbing spirits. This legend revolves around children who were either abandoned or murdered. The souls of these unbaptized children are doomed to wander the Earth, seeking someone who can provide them with a proper burial. They are believed to be particularly dangerous, possessing the ability to harm and even kill people.

The Myling's reputation as one of the most terrifying ghosts in Scandinavian folklore comes from the belief that they harbor anger and seek vengeance. The term *utburd* (meaning "that which is taken outside") has also been used to describe the practice of abandoning children in places where their chances of survival are slim. It is said that the spirits of these children will reappear either at their final resting place or, as depicted in numerous tales, in the homes of their murderers.

Legend has it that during the night Mylings will follow solitary travelers, pleading to be carried to the cemetery so that they may find eternal rest in consecrated ground. Mylings are believed to be massive beings that grow increasingly heavier as they draw nearer to a cemetery.

Eventually, they become so weighty that the person carrying them begins to sink into the soil. Should the carrier sink too deep and fail to reach the graveyard, the Myling becomes enraged and may kill them. In other versions of the tale, the Myling drains the host's energy, leaving them so exhausted that they are unable to complete the task, further enraging the spirit and sealing their own fate.

These spirits yearn for a proper burial in hallowed ground. Another belief suggests that once these children's bodies are discovered and laid to rest appropriately, they will not return as ghosts but instead find eternal peace.

If you go on a long walk in the woods and hear a baby crying in the distance, what are you going to do? I, for one, hope that you will investigate. Saving a child is one of the greatest deeds that a person can do, especially if you do it at the risk of encountering the legendary, enraged Myling.

During the thirteenth century, in a small village in Norway, a young woman named Ingrid found herself in a heartbreaking dilemma. She had succumbed to the weakness of her own heart and conceived a child out of wedlock with Ketil, the village blacksmith.

Her father, a prideful man, was livid that she had committed the sin of fornication, and even more so that it had resulted in an unwanted pregnancy. In a rage, he threatened to end her and the unborn baby's lives, declaring that the child would bring shame upon their family and lead to their exclusion from the church.

Ingrid knew deep down that her father spoke the truth. Each of these consequences was a very real possibility. Her family would suffer greatly, and once the baby was born, they would endure the most hardship. So, with Ketil's assistance, Ingrid delivered the baby in secret and together they left the newborn beneath a tall birch tree in the forest.

Tears welled in Ingrid's eyes as she walked away from the crying infant. A chilling sensation, not born of the cold, ran up her spine, shaking her to her core. Ketil wrapped his arm around her, providing solace, and guided her back to her home.

Ingrid became incessantly haunted by the cries of her baby echoing in her mind, filling her thoughts, and turning her restless dreams into terrifying nightmares. Instead of sleeping, she spent her nights staring out into the dark woods, where she believed she could still hear her child's cries amidst the labyrinth of trees and mist.

Her father grew increasingly concerned as he witnessed Ingrid's gradual withdrawal from the world. She became thinner and paler with each passing day, consumed by her sorrow. Days turned into weeks, and Ingrid spent her time by the window, always watching, always waiting.

Then, one fateful morning, her father discovered Ingrid's bed empty. Panic seized his heart as he searched desperately for his daughter. Exhausted and despondent, he eventually slumped into a chair and wept until he heard a sound—a sound emanating from the nearby woods. The sound of crying. The weeping of a young girl and the whimpering of a newborn child.

Myling

Driven by despair and an insatiable longing, Ingrid had embarked on a treacherous journey into the heart of the woods. The ancient trees whispered her name, beckoning her toward an encounter with the unknown. And there, amidst the darkness, she stood face to face with the Myling—a vengeful spirit born from the anguish of abandoned children, the anguish of her own child.

The cries of her baby resounded through the darkness, searing into Ingrid's soul. The Myling, consumed by sorrow and longing, extended its spectral arms, beckoning Ingrid closer. Overwhelmed by her desperate desire to reunite with her lost child, Ingrid surrendered herself to the creature's chilling embrace.

CHANGELING

Fairies that were left in place of a human child or newborn, whom the fairies had kidnapped, are known as changelings. There were three motives that led to the abduction of infants: to have a servant, to gain the affection of a human child from the fairies, or out of malice or revenge.

When a baby fell ill, displayed unusual physical traits, or became unable to move their limbs, the locals would often suspect fairy involvement. They referred to this condition as being "fairy-struck."

During medieval times, many of these children were abandoned or even killed because it was believed that they had been replaced by changelings.

VODYANOY

RIVER ROGUE, WATERY GUARDIAN, AND MURKY MENACE

FREAKY FACTS

LOCATION: RUSSIA

FIRST SIGHTING: OLD SLAVIC LEGENDS (DATE UNKNOWN)

CLASSIFICATION: WATER SPIRIT

PERSONALITY: CAPRICIOUS, MALEVOLENT, AND TERRITORIAL

Deep down in the dark, murky waters of Russia, there lurks unspeakable evil in the form of a toad-faced, water-dwelling, demoniacal creature. With long hair and a greenish beard dripping with slime and weeds, he looks as cantankerous as he truly is. This malevolent being is known as the Vodyanoy.

The violent and vengeful Vodyanoy is commonly sighted in lakes, ponds, rivers, and other bodies of water, but it particularly favors millponds. Within their underwater crystal palaces, illuminated by a magic stone that shines brighter than the sun, they adorn themselves with gold and silver plundered from shipwrecks. However, some choose to dwell in poor cottages made of sand and slimy wood.

The Vodyanoy take pleasure in playing card games, smoking wooden pipes, and dragging innocent victims into watery graves or enslaving their spirits. They rarely venture far from their aquatic abodes, for they are said to be powerless on dry land, yet practically invincible in water. Often, they can be seen floating in rivers and streams on half-sunken logs, making obnoxious splashes.

Beware of angering these slippery creatures, for they will break dams, destroy water mills, and drown both people and animals. Their wrath knows no bounds when provoked.

Are you planning on going for a swim in Lake Ladoga or maybe catching some pike perch in the Volga River? Put on your swimsuit and pack all your fishing gear, but don't forget to make the sign of the cross before entering the water.

Nine-year-old Alek's favorite time of the year was when his family went on vacation. This year, they went to their favorite place, the Volga River, planning to spend a week fishing, paddling, and swimming.

On the first day, it was crucial to start with some fishing. Fishing was Alek and his father's ritual. From where he stood, Alek could see his father rigging up his fishing pole. Alek himself was playing in a section of the river sheltered by a sandbar, which made it less affected by the river's fast current. He was using a small, round, metallic lure that the fish in this area seemed to enjoy. He attached the lure to the fishing line and practiced swinging it.

After only a few swings, Alek felt a sudden lightness. He looked up to see his metallic lure flying off the line and into the water just beyond the sandbar. Surprisingly, nobody else seemed to have witnessed what had occurred. Alek stood up and waded through the shallow water over the sandbar.

MÉLUSINE

Mélusine, a freshwater spirit, resides in sacred springs or rivers. She is frequently portrayed with a serpent or fishlike lower body (similar to a mermaid), and sometimes depicted with two tails. It is also believed that she possesses wings.

Folklore surrounding Mélusine can be found in various regions including Germany, France, Spain, and the British Isles. Her tale dates to the fourteenth century. When Mélusine was young, she entombed her father in a mountain, which caused great sorrow to her mother. As a consequence of her mother's disapproval, Mélusine was sentenced to transform into a serpent from the waist down every Saturday.

Peering down into the water, he could see the lure about 3 feet (1 m) away. The only problem was that the current was much stronger in this area. Alek, an overconfident child almost to the point of cockiness, didn't think twice about asking for help or considering the danger. Ignoring his father's teachings, Alek stepped into the water without hesitation. The water quickly grew deeper, reaching his chest after just a few steps.

"Alek, what are you doing!?" his father yelled from the shore. He screamed at the top of his lungs, but Alek paid no attention. He was determined to get his hands on that lure. As he waded through the water, he suddenly felt it vanish beneath the surface.

He thought he saw something looking back at him from beneath the water. It must have been a trick of the light or the green slime entangling his lure. Just as he was about to reach into the water to search for it, a hand shot out and grabbed his arm. Alek desperately tried to break free and fought with all his might, but he was no match for the force that pulled him deeper into the water.

It was cold—frighteningly, painfully cold. The river had always been chilly, but as it closed around him, Alek felt as though he was being smothered in ice. His chest felt like it would explode from the strain. A few torturous moments stretched on indefinitely as the boy struggled to breathe, but it eventually became too much. Exhaling, Alek succumbed to the depths of the water.

$$Vodyanoy$$

He felt his body being dragged down to the riverbed. Something held him there, pinned against the rocks as the water rushed past. In a panic, Alek opened his eyes and found himself staring into the eyes of a strange old man. The man had a face reminiscent of a frog, with hair floating frantically around his head, and the evilest smile gracing his lips.

The old man's sinister grin widened as Alek struggled against the invisible force that kept him trapped underwater. Panic set in as the boy realized he was in the clutches of some malevolent creature, far from the playful fish he was accustomed to encountering in the river. The old man's unnaturally strong grip seemed to tighten further, suffocating Alek.

In his mind, Alek desperately called out for his father, hoping against hope that he would hear his son's cries for help. But the rushing water muffled his voice, and the river carried his silent pleas away. The world above the water's surface seemed distant, an unreachable realm, as the Vodyanoy claimed him as its own.

WEREWOLF

EUROPE'S HOWLING, LUNAR CURSE

FREAKY FACTS

LOCATION: EUROPE

FIRST SIGHTING: SIXTEENTH CENTURY

CLASSIFICATION: CANINE – SHAPESHIFTER

PERSONALITY: FEROCIOUS, AGGRESSIVE, ANIMALISTIC, NOCTURNAL, AND CURSED

A Werewolf is an individual who, due to a curse or affliction, undergoes a transformation into a wolf during the night of a full moon, preying upon animals, humans, and even corpses. At sunrise, the Werewolf reverts to its human form.

Theoretically, genetic Werewolves—those born with a curse or inheriting a gene from one or both parents—possess the ability to change at will and can do so at any time, regardless of the hour or month. Werewolves that transform involuntarily have either been bitten or, in other cases, have contracted the curse or illness through their bloodline.

Although both types of Werewolves possess equal strength, genetic werewolves hold the advantage of surprise and opportunity since they can transform continuously for at least twenty-nine consecutive days and nights.

During the transformation, the teeth sharpen, the body becomes covered in thicker hair, the nails elongate into claws, and facial features such as the nose, eyes, and mouth enlarge. Additionally, the body gains size and bulk.

The process of transforming into a Werewolf is likely to be excruciating. In certain instances, bones rapidly expand and change shape, causing the person's skin to tear. This complete metamorphosis, which can take several minutes, gives rise to a creature that embodies a hybrid of wolf and human characteristics to varying degrees.

Werewolves are renowned for their immense strength, agility, and their ferocious teeth and claws that can effortlessly shred apart flesh. It's worth noting that even a single bite from them can prove fatal, as each tooth and claw harbors harmful pathogens that can be transmitted to surviving victims.

If a Werewolf sustains an injury while in its wolf form, the wound will manifest on its human form, potentially exposing its true identity. Some believe that due to their rapid healing and regenerative abilities, werewolves are nearly indestructible.

Numerous techniques are rumored to possess the potential to kill a werewolf, although employing a silver blade or bullet is the most commonly cited method.

In books and movies, werewolves usually meet their end by the tip of a silver bullet, and everyone lives happily ever after. However, it is probable that if a cursed werewolf were to become a menace to a small village with little means to defend themselves, the story may end very differently.

The forest was illuminated by an unsettling glow from the full, bright moon. The trees rustled in the wind, their branches reaching out like bony fingers, and the leaves whispered secrets to each other. It was the perfect night for a mysterious creature to emerge from the depths of darkness.

THE BEDBURG WEREWOLF

In the late sixteenth century, the German town of Bedburg was plagued by a reign of terror unleashed by a horrifying creature. Accused of being a Werewolf, a man named Peter met a gruesome fate. According to his own disturbing account, Peter claimed to have received a magical belt from the devil himself. To the horror of all, Peter also confessed to committing gruesome murders, taking the lives of over a dozen innocent people.

The villagers knew better than to venture into the woods on nights like these. Generations of tales had been passed down, warning them of the lurking danger. They knew that something sinister resided in the heart of the forest, something that hungered for the taste of human flesh, patiently awaiting its next victim. But, as often happens, there is always one foolhardy soul who ignores the warnings and proceeds with reckless abandon.

A young man, smitten by first love and a longing to impress his lady, set out to find the precious moonflower that only bloomed in the forest in the light of the full moon. He thought it would prove his bravery and cunning to bring her the rare gift. Adrian had heard the tales since he was a child and thought they were just stories made up to keep children out of the woods. He knew the forest well from days spent exploring with his friends. So, even if there was something menacing awaiting him, he was sure of his ability to escape.

Still ignorant of the very real danger that awaited him, Adrian walked deep into the forest. His heart pounded in his chest, filling his ears with an ominous rhythm. Every rustle, every whisper of the wind made him jump. Yet, driven by the force of love, he pressed on.

Finally, he saw it. There, in an opening filled by the moon's glow, was a white-petaled flower. The kiss of the moonlight made it sparkle and glow. Adrian stepped forward and gently plucked the single flower, cradling it in his hand.

Deeply pleased with his prize, his self-satisfaction distracted him from his surroundings. He was caught off guard when the creature emerged from the shadows, a grotesque amalgamation of man and wolf. Its eyes glowed with an unholy light, piercing the darkness. Towering over the man, it exuded an aura of primal power. Its fur, as black as the void, bristled with malevolence, and its teeth, sharp as daggers, gleamed with a thirst for blood.

Panic seized Adrian's heart, and he attempted to flee, his survival instinct kicking into overdrive. But it was too late. The werewolf, fueled by its insatiable hunger, pounced on him with ferocious speed and strength. Claws tore through flesh, and teeth sank deep into vulnerable skin. Adrian's screams for mercy echoed through the night, a futile plea in the face of relentless savagery.

As dawn broke, the villagers discovered Adrian's gnarled, lifeless body. Filled with dread and grief, they gave him an unmarked grave, hoping that by concealing his resting place, they could appease the wrath of the beast.

Little did they know that the grave wasn't enough to keep the beast at bay. The next full moon arrived, and something beastly clawed its way out of the grave.

Now there was a new wolf in the forest.

Werewolf

KELPIE

A SHAPESHIFTING, WATERY STEED WITH MURDEROUS INTENTIONS

FREAKY FACTS

LOCATION: SCOTLAND AND IRELAND

FIRST SIGHTING: 1759

CLASSIFICATION: EQUINE SHAPE-SHIFTING WATER SPIRIT

PERSONALITY: DECEPTIVE, MALEVOLENT, AND PREDATORY

Among the numerous water spirits prevalent in Celtic folklore, the Kelpie stands as one of the most renowned, said to haunt Scotland's and Ireland's lakes, rivers, and streams. Able to manifest as both a horse and a human, this shape-shifting, magical water horse harbors malicious intentions.

In its horse form, the Kelpie is adorned with a saddle and bridle to capture the attention of its victims. Intrigued by its mesmerizing allure, unsuspecting individuals are drawn toward it, tempted to mount and ride the magnificent creature.

Yet, once seated upon the saddle, they find themselves ensnared by a supernatural adhesive, unable to dismount. With its captive rider securely in place, the Kelpie gallops swiftly toward the ocean, submerging both horse and victim into its depths. There, amidst the watery abyss, the unfortunate rider meets a tragic fate—drowning and ultimately becoming a meal for the malevolent being. The Kelpie is said to discard the human entrails upon the ground, a macabre sight left for others to discover.

The Kelpie possesses the ability to assume various forms. It can take on the appearance of a mesmerizing young woman, luring unsuspecting men to their watery demise. Alternatively, it may disguise itself as a hairy human, lurking near the river's edge, ready to ensnare unwary travelers with its powerful grip.

According to certain renditions of the legend, the Kelpie exhibits distinct characteristics. Its mane is said to be composed of snakes, while its hooves face in the opposite direction. Remarkably, even when it transforms into a human form, it retains these hoof-like features. If you suspect someone may be a Kelpie, inspect their hair for water weeds—a telltale sign.

Similar to other water spirits, the Kelpie holds dominion over bodies of water and possesses the ability to conjure floods that expel intruders. According to the lore, when the Kelpie's tail submerges into the sea, it emits a thunderous sound. Whether encountered on land or in the water, the Kelpie is a formidable and perilous entity.

Some believe that if you hear wailing or howling near a body of water, exercise caution, as it may indicate a Kelpie warning others of an approaching storm.

The strength of the Kelpie is said to surpass that of ten horses, and its endurance exceeds many more. It can only be captured if it emerges without its bridle, as this piece of tack possesses magical properties. Waving or shaking the Kelpie's magic bridle toward someone can transform them into a horse or pony.

The sole reliable method to capture and control the Kelpie is when it emerges without its magical bridle through the use of another bridle marked with a cross. Once captured, one can harness its power.

There was once a small village in Scotland nestled near the banks of a winding river. The villagers led simple lives, relying on the land and water for sustenance. Life was peaceful and harmonious until an ominous presence entered their midst.

One sunny day, a young girl named Fiona found herself drawn to the riverbank. She had spent many days there wading on the river's edge looking for treasures that had washed up on the bank, but on this day she would find something she had never seen before.

As Fiona approached the river, a sight met her eyes that took her breath away. A majestic horse stood before her, its ebony coat glistening in the sunlight, and its eyes shimmering like precious gemstones.

Unable to resist the allure of the magnificent creature, Fiona's fascination overcame her fears. She mustered the courage to climb onto the horse's back, and, without warning, the horse sprang forward, galloping along the riverbank with an exhilarating speed. Fiona felt the wind whip through her hair, a symphony of freedom and thrill. She believed she had found a companion in this magnificent steed.

Yet, as their journey unfolded, an eerie transformation began to take place. The horse's mane began to writhe and hiss beneath her hands. Fiona's heart sank, realization dawning upon her with devastating clarity that this was no mere horse.

The Kelpie surged forward with such speed

Kelpie

FREAKY FOLKLORE

—

PUCA

Another strange creature from Celtic folklore is a goblin-like creature called the Puca.

The Puca (Irish for "spirit" or "ghost") is a mythical being, usually from Ireland. It is believed that they can help or harm rural and seaside communities, bringing both good and bad fortune. It is frequently depicted in animal form, such as a horse or a rabbit, and is infamous for tricking people.

The Puca is described in some tales as a friendly yet mischievous spirit, while in others it is depicted as more malevolent and capable of harming humans.

that Fiona was thrown back. Her hair whipped violently as the creature moved faster than any normal horse could. It was as though she was being carried by the wind—all she could do was hold on and pray that she would survive.

Within moments, the Kelpie had taken them into the deep, murky depths of the river. The creature seemed invigorated by the water, making strange, inhuman sounds as it swam.

Fiona tried to scream out for help, but she was completely submerged. The water was cold, and she struggled to hold her breath, her lungs burning. Her heart pounded with fear and anguish. She thrashed against the Kelpie's hold, her hands clawing at its mane, but her struggles were futile against its supernatural strength.

With a final, agonizing gasp, Fiona's body went limp. The Kelpie's grip never faltered as it continued its relentless descent into the dark abyss of the river. The water closed over them, swallowing them whole, and the world above faded from Fiona's consciousness.

BLACK SHUCK

LEGENDARY ENGLISH SPECTRAL CANINE AND HERALD OF MISFORTUNE

FREAKY FACTS

LOCATION: ENGLAND

FIRST LITERARY MENTION: 1850

CLASSIFICATION: HARBINGER OF DOOM – SPECTRAL CANINE

PERSONALITY: MALEVOLENT, MYSTERIOUS, AND OMINOUS

For centuries, the residents of East Anglia, UK, have whispered tales of a colossal black dog with fiery, malevolent eyes that supposedly roams the countryside and coastline. Its eyes are said to possess an eerie glow, appearing either red, green, or even as a single enormous red eye protruding from the center of its forehead.In some accounts, the dog is described as lacking a head, yet its eyes shine brightly in the darkness. It is sometimes depicted wearing a collar made of rattling chains.

Legends of the Black Shuck are pervasive in the folklore of Essex, Norfolk, Suffolk, and the Cambridgeshire Fens, with numerous variations of the creature's nature. Some portray it as an omen of death, while others depict it as a friendly entity.

Aside from haunting graveyards, desolate country roads, mist-laden marshes, and hills near settlements, the Black Shuck prowls the beaches. It often travels along old, straight roads or tracks believed to align with leys—invisible lines of Earth energy used by ancient peoples to locate villages and sacred sites.

On stormy nights, the Black Shuck's bone-chilling cries can be heard piercing through the howling wind. Travelers may sense its icy breath on their necks, even though the creature's footsteps make no sound and leave no trace.

Encountering or witnessing the Black Shuck is said to foretell imminent death or misfortune within a year. However, it is believed that the creature remains benign in Suffolk as long as it is left undisturbed. In certain parts of Devon, even the mention of a black dog is considered unlucky.

Not all things are as they appear. It is a curious truth that a creature, initially terrifying to behold, may bear the appearance of a monstrous being, only to reveal itself as an unexpected savior.

As the moon hung high in the night sky, casting a haunting glow over the desolate road, Thomas walked with Emily toward her house. They had spent their evening together watching scary movies, and as the hour had grown late, he insisted on walking her home.

A howl in the distance caused them both to pause their steps.

"That movie must still have me on edge," Emily said, with a nervous giggle.

"I guess for me too," Thomas replied with a laugh.

As the couple began their walk again, they heard rustling in the bushes beside the road. Something was out there, they knew for sure, but what it was they were unsure.

Suddenly, their footsteps faltered as they spotted a pair of fiery red eyes gleaming in the darkness. The eyes belonged to a towering black dog. Fear gripped Thomas and Emily, freezing them in their tracks. Heart pounding, Thomas stepped in front of Emily,

HELLHOUND

A Hellhound's presence can be discerned by a bone-chilling howl or the unmistakable stench of brimstone, especially when traversing the countryside at night. Once your eyes behold one of these horrifying apparitions, your fate is sealed, and your days are numbered.

These spectral canines far surpass the size of regular dogs. While a colossal Hellhound can tower over horses and bears, a smaller variant measures around the size of a mastiff. Their eyes emit a furious glow of red-green flames, and their fur is as dark as the depths of coal mines. The most perilous among these creatures may possess multiple heads, or even more dreadfully, lack a head altogether.

expecting the creature to pounce, its sharp fangs sinking into their flesh. Instead, it lowered its head and growled, a rumbling threat that they dare not try to pass.

The creature's presence was suffocating, causing Thomas and Emily to slowly back away. With trembling limbs, Thomas and Emily cautiously turned and resumed their journey down a different path, their minds reeling with questions and fear.

"Did that really just happen?" Thomas said. Emily remained silent, lost in her thoughts. The dog reminded her of something she had once read about.

As they walked on, the distant sound of agonized screams pierced the night. Panic surged through their veins, their hearts pounding in their chests. The cries grew louder, echoing through the darkness, chilling them to their very core.

"We have to go see what's happening. Someone could be hurt," Thomas insisted apologetically, because he could see that Emily was trembling with fear.

Driven by a mix of curiosity and dread, Thomas and Emily followed the trail of screams, their steps quickening as they approached the source of the commotion. The scene that awaited them was one of horror and tragedy. Two men lay lifeless on the road, their bodies battered and bloodied, with their wallets on the ground, emptied. Robbery had claimed their lives, leaving behind a grim reminder of the darkness that lurked in the shadows.

Black Shuck

"That could have been us," Emily said in a hushed voice.

The young couple stood there, stunned, realizing the grim fate that could have befallen them had it not been for the black dog's intervention. They would have walked down this same path, and their bodies would be lying lifeless on the roadside.

It slowly dawned upon Thomas and Emily that the creature they had encountered had not only been a harbinger of death but also a guardian in disguise.

Thomas and Emily, forever indebted to the Black Shuck, paid homage to the creature, their gratitude etched deep within their hearts. They understood that not all demons carried malice, and that even in the darkest of tales, a glimmer of salvation could be found.

NUCKELAVEE

A HUMAN-HORSE HYBRID WITH A PENCHANT FOR PESTILENCE

FREAKY FACTS

LOCATION: ORKNEY ISLANDS, SCOTLAND

FIRST LITERARY MENTION: 1759

CLASSIFICATION: EQUINE-HUMANOID HYBRID (MALEVOLENT WATER SPIRIT)

PERSONALITY: MYSTERIOUS, DESTRUCTIVE, GROTESQUE, AND MALEVOLENT

The Scottish islands harbor the most malevolent of demons, known as the Nuckelavee, which possesses no redeeming qualities. The deity called the Mither o' the Sea kept it imprisoned in the depths of the ocean during the summer months. Teran, also known as the mythical spirit of winter, engaged in a struggle for dominance against the Nuckelavee.

However, after months of repressing all evil, the exhausted Mither finally succumbed, leading to the Nuckelavee's liberation. Contrary to expectations, the Nuckelavee freely roamed the land despite the sea being considered its natural habitat. Mortals often witness this fearsome creature as it travels over land on equally fearsome steeds. The rare descriptions that have survived portray the Nuckelavee as having a head "ten times greater" than that of a man. Its single eye blazes crimson with flames, while its massive mouth juts out like the snout of a pig. These robust beings weigh about 2,000 pounds (907 kg) and stand around 6 feet (2 m) at their horselike heads and 9 feet (3 m) at their humanoid heads.

The Nuckelavee has the appearance of a horse with partially fish finlike appendages for legs. Along the horse's back, a human figure with an oversized head melds into an eerie, centaur-like creature. The most horrifying aspect of its visage is its lack of skin. Yellow veins course with black blood, while pale tendons and robust muscles pulsate ominously. Some tales mention the creature having only two small arms and two small heads, among its other peculiar traits.

Encountering such a sight along a desolate coastline would be far from pleasant. Just the sight of one of these evil creatures is enough to make anyone's blood run cold.

Finn stood at the window of his small Boston apartment, the city's sounds and lights filling his lonely existence. It had been years since he last saw his grandfather, but today, a letter arrived that would change everything. The familiar handwriting on the envelope brought back memories of his father's tales about the mystical beauty of the Orkney Islands, particularly the island of Hoy, where his grandfather lived.

Filled with a mix of curiosity and longing, Finn packed his bags and embarked on the journey to his grandfather's home. As he arrived on the Orkney Islands, the salty breeze and rugged landscape greeted him. His grandfather stood waiting at the dock, a warm smile on his weathered face, accompanied by his loyal sheepdog, Ollie. He recognized Finn right away.

"You look like your father," he said, as he embraced his grandson with a surprisingly strong hug.

Later, over dinner, Finn's grandfather confessed that he was growing old and could no longer manage the farm alone. He looked at Finn with a mixture of hope and

NIX

In Germanic and Scandinavian folklore, Nixes are water sprites that entice humans to enter the water. While some myths portray Nixes as malevolent entities, others present them as benign and helpful creatures.

Defining the true appearance of male Nixes is challenging due to their shape-shifting abilities, which allow them to assume various forms. When they take on human forms, they can be identified by the damp hems of their garments.

apprehension, offering him the chance to stay and help. Finn hesitated, knowing he had a life waiting for him in Boston, but the allure of his roots and the island's enchantment were hard to resist. He agreed to stay for two weeks, testing the waters of farm life.

In the following days Finn immersed himself in the routines of tending to the farm. His grandfather shared stories of the land's secrets, including the existence of Mortasheen, a disease that plagued the sheep during the winter months. He spoke in hushed tones of the Nuckelavee, a terrifying water demon said to be the source of the illness.

One cold morning, as they ventured out to check on the sheep, they discovered three of the flock lifeless on the ground. The earth was too frozen to bury the bodies, so they gathered wood and prepared to burn them. In the distance, Finn heard eerie noises, the sound of hooves, and guttural growls. His heart raced as he caught a glimpse of the hideous creature approaching. With fear gripping them, he and his grandfather rushed into the safety of the barn, slamming the door shut.

Hours turned into restless minutes as they waited in the dimly lit barn, the sounds of the Nuckelavee's enraged snarls piercing the night. Suddenly, a crash, a splash, and a bloodcurdling scream echoed through the air.

Finn and his grandfather looked at each other, dread filling their hearts. They knew the Nuckelavee had claimed another victim. The scream had come from Ollie, the loyal sheepdog that had been guarding the farm. Finn's grandfather grabbed his shotgun and headed out, determination etched on his face. Finn followed him, not willing to let his grandfather face the demon alone.

Nuckelavee

As they stepped out, the cold wind cutting through their bones, they saw the Nuckelavee by the shore, its back to them. The creature was a grotesque sight: It looked like a human torso had become fused to the back of a horse. The entire beast appeared to be skinless, baring yellow veins that were pulsing with black blood.

The Nuckelavee, a monstrous amalgamation of horse and rider, charged back into the ocean, and disappeared from sight. They had narrowly escaped the clutches of the Nuckelavee, but the encounter left an indelible mark on Finn's soul. Determined to protect his grandfather and honor their legacy, Finn made a solemn promise to remain by his side and tend to the farm.

OGRE

MONSTROUSLY REPULSIVE AND HABITUALLY HUNGRY

FREAKY FACTS

LOCATION: UNITED KINGDOM
(ESPECIALLY LONDON), AS WELL
AS PARTS OF ASIA AND AFRICA

FIRST SIGHTING: SEVENTEENTH
CENTURY

CLASSIFICATION: SUPERNATURAL
MONSTROUS BEING

PERSONALITY: MALEVOLENT,
BRUTISH, VIOLENT, CUNNING,
GREEDY, AND INSATIABLY
HUNGRY

Ogres, a race of repulsive monsters, once inhabited the United
Kingdom while commoners strolled the cobblestone alleys
of London. These horrifying creatures were known for their
preference for consuming young children and newborns.

The Etruscan god Orcus is often credited with the invention of the word "ogre," which has its origins in the French language. While it is unlikely that Orcus is the actual source of these monsters, his ferocious characteristics and cannibalistic tendencies were enough to establish a connection that has persisted from the late twelfth century to the present.

The origins of Ogres remain unknown, although they seem to be closely related to mythical giants and cannibals.

Ogres are always depicted as very large. Although they have a humanlike appearance, their stature clearly distinguishes them from true humans. They are often described as extremely stout and towering, evoking thoughts of giants. Ogres are known for their robust and solid bodies, which may be attributed to the abundance of muscles that contribute to their height.

In addition to their physical features, ogres are frequently described as having an excessive amount of hair. This adds to their fierce and animalistic appearance, further accentuating their intimidating nature. Furthermore, it has been observed that most of these creatures possess skin tones distinct from those of humans. Green and blue are the most commonly mentioned colors.

Ogres are infamous for their insatiable appetite for human flesh. They are terrifying creatures feared by all, but especially dreaded by mothers of young children and newborns. Ogres are notorious for rampaging through villages, leaving death and devastation in their wake due to their voracious consumption of flesh.

Ogres are mean and nasty creatures, and their cravings for a human meal make them extraordinarily terrifying. A run in with an Ogre would most likely not end well.

In the outskirts of London, there once was a dense forest that held a terrible secret. Deep within its ancient trees and hidden pathways dwelled a fearsome beast. This monstrous creature had slept undisturbed for centuries, its insatiable hunger for children kept at bay. That was until two curious kids, Lucy and Tom, stumbled upon the monster's lair.

Lucy and Tom were adventurous friends who loved exploring the woods near their homes. One sunny afternoon, fueled by their youthful curiosity, they decided to

Ogre

venture deeper into the forest than ever before. Little did they know that their innocent exploration would awaken the beast that lurked within.

As they ventured further, the air grew thick with an unnatural stillness. The once vibrant woods became shrouded in a haunting silence. Suddenly, a low growl echoed through the trees, sending a shiver down their spines. They exchanged worried glances but pressed on, unaware of the danger that awaited them.

In a secluded clearing, they stumbled upon a moss-covered stone slab, seemingly untouched by time. Drawn to its mysterious aura, the children couldn't resist the temptation to uncover its secrets. With trembling hands, they brushed away the layers of dirt, revealing a hidden inscription.

Unbeknownst to them, the inscription was a warning—a plea from the past to leave the slumbering Ogre undisturbed. But their youthful curiosity prevailed, and they recited the words aloud, unknowingly invoking the awakening of the creature.

Suddenly, the ground shook beneath them, and the forest came alive with malevolence. From the depths of the undergrowth, a large hairy Ogre emerged, towering

TROLL

Creatures of Scandinavian origin, Trolls have been depicted in vastly different ways. In Norse mythology, Trolls are hulking, giant, humanoid monsters that dwell deep in the wilderness of Scandinavia. They are aggressive, tribal giants that inhabit caves and mountains. Their appearance ranges from monstrous to eccentric to cute, but regardless of their charm, they are almost always unfriendly. Trolls reside in isolated areas such as rocks, mountains, or caves, and rarely offer assistance to human beings.

Ogres and Trolls are often mistaken for one another due to their size and frightening appearance. Both are malevolent creatures with a penchant for evil acts and a taste for human flesh. However, there are distinct differences in their behaviors and appearances that differentiate them in myth. Ogres are larger and have green skin, while Trolls tend to be smaller with gray or brown skin. Ogres prefer meat for their diet, whereas Trolls primarily consume fruits and vegetables.

over them with its hulking frame and menacing glare. Its grotesque features and jagged teeth sent waves of terror through the children's bodies.

Realizing their grave mistake, Lucy and Tom turned to flee, but it was too late. The Ogre, ravenous from its long slumber, lunged forward, its powerful arms snatching them up in an instant. Their desperate cries for help were muffled by the Ogre's monstrous grip.

As the sun began to set, darkness descended upon the forest, concealing the grisly fate of the two children. No one in the nearby town knew of the Ogre's existence, and their disappearance remained a mystery.

Within the depths of its lair, the Ogre feasted upon its prey. Its insatiable hunger sated, it retreated once more into hibernation, leaving no trace of its existence. The forest returned to its tranquil state, oblivious to the tragedy that had unfolded within its ancient embrace.

Months passed, and Lucy and Tom became mere whispers in the memories of their families and friends. The townsfolk continued their lives, unaware of the lurking danger that resided so close to their homes. The Ogre's secret remained hidden, buried within the depths of the forest, waiting for the next unsuspecting trespasser.

BABA YAGA

A CUNNING WITCH WITH A DUAL NATURE

FREAKY FACTS

LOCATION: RUSSIA

FIRST LITERARY MENTION: 1759

CLASSIFICATION: WITCH –
BOGEYMAN

PPERSONALITY: ANTAGONISTIC,
POWERFUL, CAPRICIOUS, WISE,
AND CUNNING

One of the most infamous witches in Slavic folklore, Baba Yaga is also one of the most perplexing. Will she be a friend or a foe when you encounter her?

According to a Russian folktale, Baba Yaga appears as an old lady who flies through the air in a mortar, using a pestle to steer. As she flies, she sweeps away her tracks with a broom made of silver birch, leaving behind the imprints of her pestle swipes. She may also use her pestle to crush the bones of her victims before cooking and consuming them.

The Slavic witch is depicted as an ancient, withered woman. She has iron teeth, a long and crooked nose, and bony legs. Every part of her body, including her eyes, ears, feet, hands, and mouth, is seen as ugly. She commands a strong and fiercely tempestuous personality, inspiring both respect and dread from all who encounter her.

Her dwelling resembles more of an animal than a home, with slender chicken legs that allow it to swiftly move through the forest, eluding anyone in search of the witch. The fence posts that surround Baba Yaga's hut are constructed from ancient human bones, and the bright windows serve as its watchful eyes, keeping an eye out for intruders. Atop each fence post rests a human skull, serving as a deterrent to those passing by.

As soon as visitors arrive at the hut, Baba Yaga presents them with a direct question: "Did you come here of your own free will, or were you sent?" There is only one correct response to this question: "I am here 75 percent of my own free will, 65 percent by compulsion." Those who are blessed or have pure hearts are immune to Baba Yaga's influence. Being blessed implies the protection of a mother's blessing, while being pure of heart suggests that the visitor is shielded by the power of love or virtue.

Inside her home, Baba Yaga can often be seen sprawled across her massive stove, which stretches from one side of the hut to the other. This highlights her size and power, and she sometimes barely fits inside, with her feet in one corner and her head in the other.

Baba Yaga stories frequently feature references to the stove, as failure to complete certain tasks may result in the punishment of being cooked and eaten.

Reminiscent of Hansel and Gretel, stumbling upon a creepy cabin in the woods may be a bad omen. Those who enter the witch's lair don't usually make it out with their lives.

Galina Sokolova, along with her husband Ivan and their small son Viktor, had made the Crimean Forest their home for the past four summers, when the family physician ordered her husband to spend the summer in the mountains due to his respiratory issues.

They thought they knew every hidden secret the forest held, until one evening when Ivan and Viktor were late returning from their daily hike.

As the day grew late, Galina became worried and decided to go look for them. She started down the trail in the direction they had told her they were going. Not far into the hike, she found Viktor's red sneaker lying on the forest floor. She picked up the shoe and a shiver ran down her spine. Pushing forward, she continued into the forest until she found an opening that revealed a strange cabin she had never seen before. It stood peculiarly on chicken leg–like stilts, and its roof was made of branches heavy with pine needles.

Suddenly, Galina felt like she was caught in the middle of a fairy tale–like nightmare. Memories of the tale of Baba Yaga from her childhood flooded her mind. She noticed then that the fence surrounding the cabin seemed to be made of bones, and the torches illuminating the scene were skulls—human skulls.

As she took in the eerie sight, her breath caught when she heard the whimpering of a child. Viktor? Without hesitation, she flung the cabin door open and rushed inside, driven by the single thought of rescuing her family from whatever evil had brought them there.

The dimly lit room was filled with the flickering light of candles. In one corner, there was a long iron stove and a table, and across from the table was a wooden door. The whimpering continued, and Galina knew it was coming from behind that door. She was about to reach for it when the front door creaked open.

Galina quickly dove beneath the table, attempting to make herself as small as possible. From her hiding spot, she watched as a large crone of a woman entered the cabin. Her scalp was covered by scaly skin with patches of yellowing white hair, and she had bloodshot red eyes, devoid of pupils.

"Who is here?" the crone suddenly asked. "No need to hide, my dear. I can smell my next meal from a mile away."

She continued. "You smell like the others. You can join your husband and son in their cage, and I will prepare to have three for dinner instead of two. That is good. I am so, so hungry." The witch then let out a cackle that rivaled the sound of a thousand bats.

The witch walked around the table and seized Galina by the collar. "There you are!"

Galina fought as hard as she could, but the witch effortlessly dragged her through the door and tossed her into an iron cage next to Ivan and Viktor.

Galina, Ivan, and Viktor were never seen again, their fate unknown to the world. Yet legend has it that if you venture into the depths of the Crimean Forest, you might

Baba Yaga

catch a faint echo of a child's laughter drifting through the trees. The forest holds its secrets tightly, guarding the chilling tale of the Sokolov family and the wicked crone who devoured them whole.

STRZYGA

THE UNDEAD, SLAVIC BLOODSUCKER WITH FEATHERS

FREAKY FACTS

LOCATION: POLAND AND UKRAINE

FIRST SIGHTING: PREDATES WRITTEN HISTORY

CLASSIFICATION: VAMPIRIC DEMON SHAPESHIFTER

PERSONALITY: MALEVOLENT, NIGHTMARISH, AND PREDATORY

Strzyga, a monster bearing resemblance to vampires but far more sinister in many ways, is said to exist in Polish folklore.

According to folklore, Strzyga were believed to be females who were born with two souls, two hearts, and two sets of teeth, with the second set barely noticeable. People who exhibited symptoms of sleepwalking or had hairless underarms were also considered to be Strzyga. Furthermore, the presence of teeth in a newborn baby was seen as an indication of being a Strzyga.

Once identified as Strzyga, the creatures were driven out of human settlements. During times of epidemics, people were mistakenly buried alive, and those who managed to escape their graves—often weak, sickly, and with amputated hands—were branded as Strzyga by others. It was believed that Strzyga died at a young age, but only one of their two souls was thought to move on to the afterlife. The remaining soul was believed to bring the deceased Strzyga back to life, driving them to feed on other living beings. Another belief stated that if a person's corpse was not properly treated, it could reanimate into a demonic form, emerging from the grave as a furious and murderous Strzyga.

They were said to attack nighttime travelers and people venturing into the woods after dark, sucking their blood and devouring their insides. According to legends, these undead creatures would take the form of an owl as they soared through the night.

In accordance with traditional Slavic tales, Strzyga retains memories of her previous human life. As a result, she relentlessly pursues those who mocked or harmed her in any way during her human existence.

At first, an individual affected by Strzyga may appear normal, perhaps with slightly bluish skin. However, they soon develop owl-like characteristics such as feathered wings, elongated pointed ears, and razor-sharp claws. These features, combined with their two sets of sharp teeth, make them formidable predators—predators that prey on humans.

For a brief period, it was believed that Strzyga could be satisfied with animal blood. However, other accounts suggest that Strzyga were seen as harbingers of impending death rather than inflicting physical harm on humans.

She hides in plain sight, hidden like a chameleon among the familiar faces you encounter. Yet, she is unmistakably distinct. Possessing wings, talons, and an additional row of razor-sharp teeth, she lurks out there, somewhere, prowling for blood and entrails. Beware, for tonight she may be on the hunt, and you could be her chosen prey.

Wyatt led a simple life as an ordinary high school student, immersed in basketball and hanging out with his friends. Little did he know that his existence would take a sharp

Strzyga

turn when his orphaned cousin, Daria, arrived from Poland to live with his family following the sudden demise of her parents.

Their first encounter took place when Wyatt caught Daria snooping around his bedroom after school. However, their initial awkwardness swiftly transformed into a genuine friendship. Though Wyatt was intrigued by Daria's mysterious aura, he couldn't help but feel that there was something peculiar about her. Daria confided in him about her unique condition: She had been born with a full set of teeth, and a second row that emerged at the age of two.

"That is weird," he remembered saying, regrettably, later.

Wyatt's friends were instantly smitten by Daria's stunning appearance and enigmatic aura, except for his ex-girlfriend, Cassie. Cassie, harboring resentment, pretended to befriend Daria and invited her for a supposedly friendly ice-skating outing on the local pond. However, Cassie's true intentions were far from innocent. She callously pushed Daria onto thin ice, jeopardizing her life as Daria fell through, struggling to survive the bone-chilling waters.

Following Daria's recovery from the hospital, Wyatt noticed increasingly peculiar attributes about her. He observed the abnormally long length of her nails, her propensity for extended periods of sleep, and the mysterious presence of an owl perched on her window whenever she was absent from her room.

The strangeness escalated when Cassie's friends began experiencing inexplicable, brutal deaths. They were discovered with their throats viciously torn and their bodies grotesquely split from sternum to groin, devoid of any entrails.

"Is it possible Daria could be responsible for this? Is it somehow revenge?" He quietly asked himself out loud one night while lying in bed. He shook his head, brushing it off as paranoia, yet he couldn't shake the feeling that he was right.

In memory of the slain friends, the entire class planned to meet and build a bonfire at the very pond where the ice-skating accident had occurred. On the evening of the meeting, fate would intertwine with truth, unmasking the enigma that surrounded Daria.

In a nightmarish revelation, she transformed into a fearsome creature known as a Strzyga—a monster born from darkness and bloodlust. With deadly intent, she embarked on a merciless killing spree, sparing only Wyatt from her wrath.

"Why, Daria? They weren't all guilty of hurting you!" Wyatt pleaded with her, trying to get her to stop.

Amid the chaos and terror that unfolded, Wyatt stood as the lone survivor, witnessing the horrifying metamorphosis of his cousin. Gripped by shock and grief, he grappled to comprehend the reality of the monster Daria had become, and why she had spared him to suffer with the memory of what she had done. Was his punishment to bear the burden of the truth, which was a fate worse than death?

EL CUCUY

NOCTURNAL STEALER OF MISBEHAVING CHILDREN

FREAKY FACTS

LOCATION: SPAIN AND
PORTUGAL

FIRST LITERARY MENTION: 1274

CLASSIFICATION: BOGEYMAN

PERSONALITY: TERRIFYING,
MYSTERIOUS, NIGHTMARISH,
AND PUNITIVE

Scaring children into good behavior or dissuading them from making
bad decisions has long been a common theme in folklore around
the world. In Spain and Portugal, you may come across stories of a
bogeyman known as El Cucuy, also referred to as Coco or Coca.

    El Cucuy, the Spanish equivalent of the bogeyman, preys on
disobedient children. He seemingly materializes out of thin air
to kidnap, torture, and even devour children who refuse to heed
their parents' warnings.

The name El Cucuy originated in European Spanish-speaking countries. In these regions, the word *coco* typically means "coconut." However, it is sometimes used as a metaphor for a human head or skull.

This metaphor helps explain the other names of El Cucuy, referring to his physical appearance: skin the color of a coconut shell and a thick mane of gray hair. Additionally, El Cucuy is often depicted with large bat-like ears, glowing red eyes, razor-sharp teeth, and long, menacing claws. It is believed that he possesses an uncanny ability to hear the cries of children from miles away.

According to legend, El Cucuy can also shapeshift and assume the form of a faceless shadow, a dark and dangerous entity. He possesses a strong determination that allows him to hide in closets and under beds for extended periods.

With strength and agility, El Cucuy is a formidable presence once you become his target. It is said that you may be able to ward him off with religious symbols, such as a cross or holy water. It is said that he attacks and abducts misbehaving children. Parents have utilized this cautionary tale as a means to frighten their children, warning them of the dire consequences that will befall them if they fail to listen.

When a child misbehaves, El Cucuy will silently enter their room and conceal himself, patiently waiting for the child to be alone. From his hiding spot, he bides his time for an opportune moment to strike.

Every parent has those moments when they wish someone would just come and take their kids for a while, but what if you were so frustrated and tired that you wished them away . . . for good?

Leslie had been a good mother, or at least she tried to be. She would drop everything to be there for her kids whenever they needed something. She sacrificed her time, money, and, most recently, her sanity for them.

Erica, her sixteen-year-old daughter, and Bryson, her fourteen-year-old stepson, were homeschooled. They made this decision in the spring of 2020 during the Covid-19 crisis, when schools were closed due to quarantine.

Everything was fine at first, but gradually things began to change. They started staying up later and later after their parents had gone to bed, breaking the rules set by Leslie and Jackson, her husband.

This morning was the breaking point. Leslie had set her alarm for 5 a.m. to meet a deadline before departing for a business trip in the morning at 10. She needed complete silence in the house to record an oral report. However, when she got up, she found both kids watching TV in the living room.

Erica burst into tears when Leslie lambasted them for staying up all night. Erica explained that she had watched a horror movie and was too scared to sleep, so she had asked Bryson to stay up with her.

This time, Leslie had no sympathy. Tired and frustrated, she told her daughter that she should be afraid because she would be lucky if El Cucuy did not come and drag her away for her constant disobedience. Erica hung her head and sobbed as she turned, raced upstairs to her bedroom, and slammed the door. Bryson followed in silence.

After the two teenagers disappeared up the stairs, Leslie, struggling to keep her rage in check, muttered under her breath, "El Cucuy can take you both for all I care. Maybe then I'll be able to have at least one peaceful day."

Leslie turned off the television and went to the kitchen to make a cup of coffee before heading down to her office. As she walked back through the living room, a heavy thump came from upstairs, just above her head. It sounded like it came from Erica's room. Leslie shook her head and sat down to listen until she was certain the kids were in bed.

El Cucuy

When she heard a loud crash from upstairs, she almost spilled her coffee. Leslie set down the mug and headed upstairs, thinking that if Erica was throwing a fit, she would make sure it was the last time.

She thought she heard crying as she approached the upstairs hallway, but Erica's pouting didn't usually go on for this long. Leslie's conscience began to sting with concern. When she got to Erica's door, she could still hear a faint cry coming from the other side.

"Erica, can I come in?" she asked softly, but there was no reply.

She slowly opened the door, surprised that it wasn't locked. The first thing she noticed was that Erica wasn't in her bed. She was about to call out to her again when she caught movement from the corner of her eye. Turning, she saw Erica lying in the closet with a gnarled, clawed hand covering her mouth.

Leslie screamed, "Erica!" and ran for her daughter, but it was too late.

She was gone, vanished beneath a pile of clothing. Falling to her knees, Leslie began frantically digging through the clothes until she found her.

Leslie's heart stopped when she looked right into the terrified face of her daughter. Her skin was pale, and she had dark rings under her eyes with tears running down her cheeks. She cried, "Momma," but the word was smothered by wicked laughter.

Erica reached out with both hands in desperation, but as Leslie grabbed her hands and began to pull, large, clawed hands wrapped around her daughter's face on both sides and pulled her into the closet, where she disappeared into the darkness forever.

AFRICA

There are many strange, unusual, and frightening animals in Africa, as well as in African folklore. Animals and tricksters frequently appear in most traditional folklore. These tales are not only fun to read, but they also convey valuable lessons, sometimes of a moral nature and sometimes related to survival. Written accounts of African mythology first emerged in the early 1800s, coinciding with the arrival of European explorers and colonizers. Prior to the colonial era, these stories, and the creatures in them, were usually transmitted orally from generation to generation.

TOKOLOSHE

THE GOBLIN-SIZED ZULU TRICKSTER

FREAKY FACTS

LOCATION: SOUTH AFRICA

FIRST SIGHTING: PREDATES
WRITTEN HISTORY

CLASSIFICATION: DWARFLIKE
SPIRIT

PERSONALITY: MISCHIEVOUS,
NOCTURNAL, AND MALEVOLENT

Zulu mythology describes a creature called the Tokoloshe that is said to live in South Africa. These creatures are responsible for the practice of elevating mattresses off the ground among many Zulu people, as Tokoloshes are believed to attack people while they sleep. The apparition also appears in Bantu folklore to explain why people die inexplicably while sleeping in their rondavels at night.

The Tokoloshe is depicted as a shriveled, hairy humanoid resembling a dwarf. It may have sunken eyes and often sports a hole in its forehead, giving it a zombie, poltergeist, or gremlin-like appearance. It is said to be agile, somewhat ghostly, and has a fondness for curdled milk.

These creatures are regarded as vile and highly dangerous. It is rumored that they sneak into people's bedrooms while they are sound asleep, causing havoc by frightening or even strangling them with their long, bony fingers. Some believe that the Tokoloshe may even feed on human blood. They are known to leave deep scratches on the bodies of children and delight in instilling fear in them.

According to legend, this cunning creature from South Africa is held responsible for a wide range of misfortunes, including theft, divorce, and, at times, even fatalities. While most people have never claimed to have seen a Tokoloshe, it is widely believed that if anything goes wrong or unusual occurrences take place in South African households, the Tokoloshe is blamed as the cause.

It is said that the only way to escape its deadly curse is to sleep in an elevated position. But what if you don't have any other choice but to sleep on the floor?

Unfortunate circumstances had forced Zuri to bid farewell to her beloved hometown and childhood friends. A month ago, her father had fallen ill, his condition baffling the doctors in Montagu. They traced the source of his sickness to a mysterious bite on his ankle, which had become infected. Though the bite had seemingly healed, her father's health had steadily declined, his nights plagued by feverish torment and days marred by debilitating weakness.

In search of specialized treatment, Zuri's family had relocated to Durban, moving in with her grandmother. While the house itself was modest yet comfortable, Zuri had lost the luxury of her own room—a privilege she had taken for granted during her sixteen years. Sharing a cramped space with her parents proved challenging. Her makeshift mattress in the corner barely accommodated her, forcing her to curl up to prevent her feet from dangling over the edge and onto the floor.

The situation was made worse by her suspicion of rats infesting her grandmother's home. She had experienced the unsettling sensation of something scurrying over her during the night on multiple occasions. Later, as Zuri lay in bed, attempting to drift off to sleep, she overheard her mother's tearful conversation with her grandmother. Intrigued, she ventured out of her bed and stealthily approached the kitchen, eavesdropping from the shadows.

Amidst the hushed tones, her mother spoke of a peculiar tale. "It must have followed us here. I believed that by leaving it would lose track of us. Someone must have cursed him to suffer such a torment. We must find a way to stop it before it claims his life."

Her grandmother responded with a raspy voice, "A shaman is our only hope—a skilled healer capable of banishing the Tokoloshe."

A creaking floorboard beneath her feet startled Zuri, causing the two women to lower their voices. She pondered the nature of their conversation, realizing that the Tokoloshe—once dismissed as a mere childhood legend—held a deeper, sinister significance.

Recalling the unsettling sounds she had heard earlier in her bedroom, Zuri grew apprehensive about returning to bed. Seeking an excuse, she casually strolled into the kitchen, feigning a need for a glass of water. Her mother's reaction was expected, shooing her back to her room.

Nervous yet resolute in her determination to protect her father from further harm, Zuri settled onto her mattress, clutching a book for distraction as she tried to stay awake all night.

Tokoloshe

FREAKY FOLKLORE

As she delved into the pages, losing herself in the story's narrative, the lights flickered before extinguishing. Holding her breath, Zuri anxiously awaited their return, but minutes passed with no sign of the power resuming. Realizing she needed candles, she hesitated, loath to leave her father alone in the darkness. However, his peaceful slumber and the urgency to retrieve the light compelled her to take action.

With trepidation, Zuri took two hesitant steps, only to freeze at the sound of scurrying across the floor. She fought the instinct to flee as her leg abruptly collided with an obstacle, tiny claws digging into her ankles. Toppling over, books flew from her grasp as she crashed onto the floor, gasping for breath.

When she finally managed to inhale, terror struck her core as she beheld a sight that would forever haunt her. A short, hairy creature—roughly the size of a cat—clambered onto her chest. Zuri remained paralyzed with fear, her gaze locked onto the empty sockets that should have held eyes. She yearned to move, to escape, but the weight of terror restrained her. As her heart pounded against her chest, life gradually returned to her limbs, but it was too late. The nightmarish creature clasped its hands around her throat, its sharp claws piercing her skin.

ADZE

A SHAPESHIFTING VAMPIRIC CREATURE THAT HIDES IN HUMAN FORM

FREAKY FACTS

LOCATION: WEST AFRICA

FIRST SIGHTING: PREDATES
WRITTEN HISTORY

CLASSIFICATION: VAMPIRIC
SHAPESHIFTING INSECTOID

PERSONALITY: BLOODTHIRSTY,
DECEPTIVE, MYSTERIOUS,
MALEFIC, AND MALEVOLENT

In African folklore, insects are popular creatures because they are
often used to teach moral lessons or serve as warnings against the
dangers of the world.

One such creature that takes the form of a firefly is the Adze,
found in Togo and Ghana. The Adze is a vampiric being that preys
on men and women, but it seems to have a preference for children.

Although the Adze typically appears as a firefly, it can change into a human form once captured. In its human form, it possesses the power to take control of regular humans and even turn them into witches.

Different circumstances may lead to suspicions of Adze possession. A woman with brothers, particularly if their offspring have achieved greater success than her own, or an elderly person if the young people around them start dying unexpectedly while they remain unharmed, could be indications of Adze possession. Poor individuals who hold envy for the wealthy may likewise be under suspicion.. The Adze serves as a warning against the dangers of envy for people of all ages. If you envy your brother or neighbor, the Adze may pass through a closed door at night and feed on your and your family's blood as you all sleep. The Adze doesn't drain its victims completely, but the victim will fall ill and eventually succumb to death.

You may wonder how anyone could be afraid of anything as magical as a tiny, glimmering firefly. But in Africa, it is known by the young and old that evil can come in many forms, even that of a tiny, little bug.

It was a starless night. The village was shrouded in darkness, broken only by the occasional rustle of leaves dancing in the wind. All the villagers in Watamu were fast asleep, their dreams undisturbed by the world outside—all except one.

Young Kofi lay in his bed, his eyes fixed on the ceiling. Sleep eluded him, his thoughts returning to the events that had unfolded earlier that evening. Kofi's aunt didn't like him, and he didn't understand why. He had gone to her home and asked if he could try to cheer up his cousin, who was sick. However, she told him to get out and slammed the door in his face.

His father had told him that she was jealous because her son was sickly, while Kofi was vibrant and strong. That made no sense to Kofi; he couldn't help his cousin's circumstances.

A sudden noise shattered the stillness, originating from outside his window. Kofi sat up, his gaze drawn to the source. A firefly floated in the air, its wings softly flapping,

ASANBOSAM

In Togo and Ghana, there exists a species of vampire known as the Asanbosam that is often found lurking in the trees. Suspended by its curved legs, it patiently waits for unsuspecting passersby. Once someone walks beneath its perch, the Asanbosam seizes them, using its sharp iron teeth to sever their throat and feed on their blood while firmly holding them in its grasp.

casting a faint glow. For a moment, he observed the tiny creature, its light flickering in the night, before he settled back into bed.

Yet the unease persisted, refusing to release its grip on Kofi's senses. He knew deep down that something was amiss—that he remained under watchful eyes. His restless gaze roamed around the room, searching for any sign of an intruder, but there was nothing to be seen.

Then, a hushed voice whispered his name, causing him to tremble.

"Kofi," it murmured.

Once more, he bolted upright, his eyes darting around the room. No one was present. The voice echoed in the air, disembodied and mysterious.

"Kofi," it called out again, the sound lingering in the stillness.

His attention turned toward the window, and there, illuminated by the darkness, hovered the firefly once more. But this time, it was transforming. It grew in size, its eyes glowing a menacing shade of red, as if reflecting the depths of a fiery abyss. Its legs elongated and reached in through the window, while its wings grew larger and much louder.

Kofi's heart raced; his body was overcome with a chilling sense of dread. He recognized the creature for what it truly was: an Adze, a malevolent being of legend and nightmares, a creature that drained the blood of its victims and left them lifeless.

Fear overwhelmed him, rendering him unable to scream. The Adze swooped into his room, landing squarely on his chest. He looked into its eyes, which were strangely human, and felt a stirring of recognition. Suddenly, Kofi felt its sharp teeth puncture his tender skin, its insidious thirst draining him of his life force.

Adze

In a desperate struggle, he fought against the creature's relentless grasp, but it possessed a strength far beyond his own. The Adze mercilessly sapped the vitality from his body, reducing him to a mere vessel, devoid of life.

At dawn, Kofi's father found his lifeless form nestled in his bed.

BULTUNGIN (WEREHYENA)

THE SHAPESHIFTING MAN-HYENA HYBRID

FREAKY FACTS

LOCATION: EAST AND NORTH
AFRICA

FIRST SIGHTING: PREDATES
WRITTEN HISTORY

CLASSIFICATION: SHAPESHIFTING
HYENA

PERSONALITY: MYSTERIOUS,
DECEPTIVE, NOCTURNAL, AND
MALEVOLENT

In the region near the Horn of Africa, encompassing countries such as
Ethiopia, Somalia, and Sudan, it is said that Werehyenas roam the lands.
　　Unlike their legendary counterparts the Werewolves, Werehyenas
can take on the form of either hyenas disguising themselves as humans
or may be hyenas that have adopted human appearances.

Werehyenas are also believed to possess the ability to transform at will, aided by a magical stick or a dusting of ash. Sometimes, even the mere scent of human flesh can trigger their metamorphosis.

Since the dawn of human presence in Africa, hyenas and humans have maintained an ongoing and antagonistic relationship. These nocturnal creatures have gathered in packs, known as cackles, throughout the ages, raiding village homes, preying on children, and decimating cattle. A hyena attack is not an isolated incident but rather a familiar occurrence in rural Africa, underscoring the awareness that we are not the dominant predators in these lands.

Naturally, Werehyenas have been employed as a symbolic representation of various threats that loom beyond human settlements in African lore. They share many traits with their hyena counterparts, exhibiting strength as both solitary hunters and pack hunters, possessing an insatiable appetite, and displaying a knack for luring prey out of their natural habitats.

In rural areas, especially in those locations where the wilderness still exerts a significant influence over daily life, the belief in Werehyenas remains prevalent. There, mothers continue to recount the tales of Werehyenas to their children as they settle them in for the night, reassuring them that if they heed the warnings, the eerie sound of the beast's cackling will not be the last thing they hear.

If a scary story doesn't deter a child from disobedience, then coming face to face with a real monster will. It may also cause them to wet their bed until they are adults.

In the remote village of Nyota, a small boy named Sulayman lived with his family. The villagers told stories about a horrible creature that roamed the savanna. They said it was neither beast nor human, but a monstrous hybrid of the hyena and man that fed on the flesh of the innocent. They called it the Bultungin-Werehyena.

Sulayman was an adventurous and curious child, and he couldn't resist exploring the outskirts of the village, despite the warnings from his elders. One moonlit night, when the air was heavy with an unnatural silence, Sulayman's curiosity got the better of him.

Bultungin (Werehyena)

ABADA

A legendary creature from Central Africa is the Abada, a mysterious, unicorn-like creature. In contrast to Western unicorns, which typically have a single horn, Abadas are depicted with two curved horns. They are often described as being the size of a small donkey with a boar-like tail. According to folklore, the elusive Abada's horns are believed to possess the power to act as an antidote to poison. While it is generally regarded as a peaceful creature, anyone who attempts to subdue it runs the risk of being impaled by its formidable horns.

He sneaked out of his hut, leaving behind his sleeping family, and ventured into the wild unknown.

As he wandered deeper into the savanna, the hairs on the back of his neck stood on end. The rustling of the grass and the occasional distant howl sent shivers down his spine, but he kept going. The moon's pale light cast eerie shadows around him, and every snap of a twig sounded like the approach of a predator.

Suddenly, Sulayman heard rustling in the weeds followed by a low, guttural growl nearby. Fear embraced his heart as he turned to see a pair of glowing eyes staring back at him from the darkness. Trembling, he tried to back away, but his feet felt rooted to the spot.

The creature slowly emerged from the shadows, its gnarled and twisted form sending terror coursing through Sulayman's veins. The creature's elongated limbs and hunched back created a grotesque silhouette against the moonlit sky. Its matted fur was a patchwork of grays and browns, and its eyes burned like hot coals.

Sulayman's heart pounded in his chest as he realized he had stumbled upon the very creature he had been warned about. He mustered all his courage and turned to flee, but the creature was swift and agile. With inhuman speed, it closed the distance between them, its sharp claws extended like deadly talons.

He ran for his life, his breaths coming in ragged gasps as he weaved through the maze of grass and shrubs. The creature's growls echoed in the night. He prayed to the spirits of his ancestors to protect him from this horrifying monster.

AFRICA

Just when Sulayman thought all hope was lost, a ray of moonlight illuminated a hidden crevice in a large rock formation. With a desperate surge of energy, he darted into the crevice and squeezed himself into the narrow space, praying the creature wouldn't find him.

In the darkness, he held his breath and listened, his heart pounding in his ears. The Werehyena's growls grew fainter, and Sulayman dared to hope that he had escaped the creature's grasp. It felt like a lifetime passed as he cowered in the tight space, fearing any movement might give away his position.

Finally, the creature's cackling screams receded into the distance and the savanna was silent once more. Sulayman remained hidden until the first light of dawn touched the sky, and the village began to stir to life.

When he emerged from his hiding place his limbs were still trembling, but he was able to make his way back to the safety of his home. His family, who had been distraught when they realized he was missing that morning, were relieved to see him unharmed.

He told them of his terrifying encounter with the Werehyena and swore to never venture far from the village after dark ever again. Forever seared in his memory, he would never forget the dangers that lurked in the shadows of the savanna and how important it was to listen to his elders. Although the creature spared him that night, he might not be so lucky next time.

KAMAPPA

WHATEVER IT IS, IT'S NOT PICKY

FREAKY FACTS

LOCATION: SOUTHERN AFRICA

FIRST SIGHTING: PREDATES
WRITTEN HISTORY

CLASSIFICATION: DEITY

PERSONALITY: SHAPELESS,
GLUTTONOUS, VIOLENT, AND
MALEVOLENT

The Sotho people of Southern Africa possessed a legendary beast
called Kamappa, often referred to as Kholomodumo in modern
Sesotho. It has been described as a shapeless, ravenous creature that
eats anything living that it comes across and grows bigger and bigger
the more it eats. It utilizes its many razor-sharp tongues as weapons.

It was also described as a nocturnal beast that secretly broke into livestock pens to murder sheep, goats, and calves. Its name is claimed to mean "gaping-mouthed bush monster." It could jump or climb over 6-foot (2 m) fences while carrying prey in its mouth, and it would leave circular footprints with 2-inch (5 cm) claw marks. In the Eastern Cape's Graaff-Reinet region, kraals were repeatedly attacked, and a group of more than one hundred settlers was unable to locate the animal.

There were many theories about the monster's identity during that time, but no one ever clearly saw it. Although hyenas drag their victims, cannot leap 6-foot (2 m) fences, and howl like demons, some people thought it was a "freak" hyena.

Kamappa is the main antagonist in the story of Ditaolane, a legendary figure in Lesotho folklore. In the story, there was a horrible monster named Kamappa that ate every human in Africa except for one person: an old woman who hid when she saw what was happening and was the only one left.

Through a miraculous conception, she became pregnant without the aid of a man. She gave birth to a son who was adorned with magical amulets, whom she named Lituolone in honor of her god.

The boy grew to adulthood by nightfall. He then asked his mother why there were no other people. She told him the story of Kamappa, and he grabbed a knife and set out to find and kill the evil creature.

Unfortunately, before he could even attack, Kamappa swallowed him whole in one single gulp. Lituolone found himself unharmed inside the creature's stomach and used his knife to cut his way out.

When he tore apart the beast's stomach, thousands of others were able to escape with him, allowing Africa to be repopulated once again.

Because of this story, Kamappa is also symbolic of what holds back humanity.

If you want to go hunting for a legendary, mythical creature, make sure it isn't one that eats everything in sight, including humans, or you may become its next meal. Or, at the least, its dessert!

In a small Sotho village hidden deep in the heart of Southern Africa, there lived two best friends, Thabo and Tumi. They were inseparable, always embarking on daring adventures together. Their village was surrounded by vast, untamed wilderness, and tales of mythical creatures were woven into the fabric of their lives.

Among these legends was the dreaded Kamappa, a shapeless and ravenous beast that devoured anything living in its path, growing larger and more menacing with each meal. The creature's many razor-sharp tongues were said to be its deadliest weapons, tearing through flesh like a nightmare given life.

Thabo and Tumi were fascinated by the chilling stories they heard around the campfire at night, but they never truly believed in the existence of such a terrifying creature. That is, until one moonlit evening when an unsettling event unfolded.

As the sun slipped from the sky, casting a soft glow over the village, Thabo and Tumi decided to sneak out of their homes for a midnight escapade. Armed with nothing but their desire for excitement and adventure, they ventured into the wilderness, curious to explore the mysteries that lay beyond.

The night was thick with shadows, and the rustling of leaves caused goosebumps to spread across their skin. Despite the unsettling feeling creeping up their backs, they pressed on, eager to prove their bravery to one another. They had heard rumors of a creature lurking in the nearby forest, and the boys couldn't resist the allure of uncovering the truth.

As they delved deeper into the woods, the air seemed to grow colder, and the sounds of nocturnal creatures echoed in the distance. Thabo held a torch aloft, its flickering flames casting creepy shapes on the trees around them.

Suddenly, a chilling howl pierced the silence, causing both boys to freeze in their tracks. Their eyes darted around, searching for the source of the haunting sound. Thabo's heart pounded in his chest, and Tumi clung to his friend's arm, fear evident in his eyes.

"I—I think we should go back," Tumi stammered, his voice barely above a whisper.

But Thabo's curiosity got the better of him. "No, we can't turn back now. We have to find out if Kamappa is real," he replied, trying to sound brave despite the tremor in his voice.

As they continued, the woods seemed to close in around them, and an oppressive feeling hung in the air. Branches twisted into unnatural shapes, and the ground beneath their feet felt unnervingly soft, as if the Earth itself were alive.

Suddenly, a low growl resonated through the darkness, sending a wave of terror through the boys. They turned to run, but before they could escape, a monstrous shape emerged from the shadows.

A massive creature stood before them: a nightmare come to life. Its formless, gaping maw seemed to swallow the moonlight, leaving only darkness in its wake. Its many tongues lashed out, glinting in the faint light, and Thabo and Tumi could feel the malevolence that emanated from the creature.

Paralyzed with fear, they could do nothing but watch in horror as the monster advanced, its massive frame growing larger with each step. The legends were true, and the boys now faced the very monster they had dismissed as mere stories. The night filled with the stench of the beast's breath, and the boys knew they had made a mistake.

Suddenly Tumi tripped and landed with a thud on the ground. Thabo tried to help him up, but Tumi's ankle was injured, and couldn't hold his weight.

Desperation took hold of Thabo, and he remembered the tales of the creature's insatiable appetite. Without hesitation, he flung the torch at Kamappa, hoping to drive the beast away.

The flames danced around Kamappa's form, but to their horror, it seemed unaffected. The creature let out a bloodcurdling screech, its tongues writhing in anger. It was clear that mere fire wouldn't deter this ancient terror.

Thabo grabbed Tumi's arm and tried to pull him, but it was no use. Kamappa was too fast. The beast's razor-sharp tongues slithered out of its mouth and wrapped around poor Tumi's ankle. Thabo watched in horror as the creature mutilated his friend and then swallowed him whole.

Tumi's screams seemed to echo through the night air as Thabo made a last, desperate attempt to escape. Thabo turned and ran, his heart pounding in his ears. The forest seemed to close in around him as the boy ran blindly through the darkened woods, branches clawing at his clothes.

With every step, the ground trembled beneath him, and he could hear Kamappa's monstrous roars echoing behind him. Thabo saw the village in the distance—he was almost there—but before he could cry for help, his feet were yanked from beneath him. He watched the lights of the village disappear as he was dragged back into the forest.

IMPUNDULU

THE ELECTRIFYING BIRD OF STORMS THAT CRAVES BLOOD

FREAKY FACTS

LOCATION: SOUTH AFRICA

FIRST SIGHTING: PREDATES
WRITTEN HISTORY

CLASSIFICATION: VAMPIRIC
SHAPESHIFTER

PERSONALITY: MYSTERIOUS,
MAGICAL, AND MALEVOLENT

The Lightning Bird, or Impundulu, is a creature from Zulu folklore. It is often thought of as a spiritual entity associated with storms and lightning. The creature appears in various forms depending on the version of the legend.

In its true form, the Impundulu is said to be human-sized, whose body is covered in white feathers. It has bright red wings, red legs, and a short red tail. Interestingly, it is believed that only women have the ability to perceive its true appearance.

In other versions, it is said to display distinctive black and white plumage, often likened to that of the Hamerkop. It possesses the ability to transform into lightning, sometimes resembling a rooster, while other depictions show it with peacock feathers or a scarlet tail, beak, and legs.

Infamous for its bloodthirst and penchant for inflicting pain, the Impundulu is known to feed on animals, birds, and even humans. Its attacks, if not lethal, can result in infertility and tuberculosis in its victims. Additionally, it possesses the ability to bring forth rain, ill fortune, and promiscuity among people. It is said to have the capability of kidnapping children or stealing milk from their homes. The flapping of its wings generates thunder, while lightning can be discharged from its talons.

In rare instances, the Impundulu descends to the ground as lightning and lays its eggs there. One can either capture the egg as soon as it touches the earth or locate it in an underground cavern where it falls, often indicated by the presence of fairy rings, which serve as markers of its impact.

Impundulu can also serve as familiars to witches and can be passed down from mother to daughter due to their immortality. However, when a witch fails to pass down her Impundulu, it becomes an untamed force of chaos and destruction. While acting as a familiar, it may be dispatched to eliminate the witch's enemies. Nonetheless, if not adequately nourished, it poses a threat to the witch's life.

The Impundulu is often seen riding on the backs of hyenas, which serve as the shapeshifting witch's alternate form.

Both the body and eggs of the Impundulu possess potent magical properties. While the eggs are often destroyed, they can be combined with other substances to create a potion that invokes lightning upon an enemy. The fat of the Impundulu can be utilized for medicinal purposes, and its flesh can serve to identify thieves. Notably, the Impundulu is vulnerable to fire, making the acquisition of these elements a challenging task.

A man-sized bird that can produce lightning, has an insatiable lust for blood, and is controlled by a witch is undoubtedly a terrifying creature. The young woman in the next story finds out the hard way that if you don't want to feel the wrath of this beast, you better not anger its master.

A young girl named Nomvula lived in the center of the Zulu tribe, tucked away in the thick, unforgiving jungles. She was known for her beauty and her keen interest in the ancient arts of the tribe. As she came of age, whispers of her remarkable abilities reached the ears of the village's witch doctor, Sauda.

Sauda, a powerful and mysterious figure in the tribe, had grown increasingly jealous of the attention Nomvula was receiving from the villagers. She feared that her burgeoning abilities would overshadow her own influence, and a seed of darkness took root within her heart.

One night, as the moon hung low in the sky, Sauda summoned her familiar, the Impundulu, a creature she had long used to serve her selfish desires. The Impundulu appeared in the form of a large bird but immediately changed into a strikingly handsome man, with enchanting eyes that held an unnerving glint of malevolence.

"Nomvula poses a threat to me," Sauda hissed, her voice tainted with envy. "I want you to seduce her, lure her into the forest, and drain her of her blood. Only then will my power be secure."

The Impundulu, bound to obey his master's command, ventured into the village under the guise of the handsome stranger. His charm was undeniable, and as he weaved through the shadows, he set his sights on Nomvula.

Under the moon's bewitching glow, Nomvula encountered the captivating stranger. Mesmerized by his alluring presence, she felt an irresistible pull toward him. The Impundulu knew precisely how to manipulate her emotions, sowing seeds of infatuation and desire within her innocent heart.

Nomvula was enamored by the stranger's charm and beauty. He spoke with a silky voice that made her skin flush, and his touch was electric. He promised her a world of passion and pleasure unlike anything she had ever experienced before. Powerless to resist his seduction, Nomvula followed him deep into the forest.

As they walked, the Impundulu's façade began
to slip, and his true form was revealed. Nomvula
recoiled in horror as the handsome stranger
transformed into a monstrous bird, with
razor-sharp claws and a screeching cry
that echoed through the jungle.

Nomvula tried to run, but the
Impundulu was too quick. He
swooped down and grabbed
her in his talons, carrying
her high into the air.
Nomvula screamed
as she felt the cold
night wind whipping
through her hair, and
she thought she was
going to die. But suddenly, the Impundulu
began to lose his grasp, and Nomvula fell from
his grip, landing on the ground next to a hut.

She could hear the Impundulu's wings
flapping as he began to descend in pursuit of her.
Frantically, she looked around for something to
fight back with. That's when she saw the torch burning next to the door of the hut. She
reached and grabbed it from its perch. With the torch in hand, Nomvula spun around to
face the Impundulu. The monstrous bird was closing in, its razor-sharp claws extended,
ready to strike. Nomvula held the torch up high, ready to defend herself.

As the Impundulu swooped down to attack, Nomvula swung the torch with all her
strength. The flames caught the creature's feathers, setting them ablaze. The Impundulu
screeched in agony and retreated into the shadows. Nomvula breathed a sigh of relief,
grateful to have escaped the monster's clutches, at least this time.

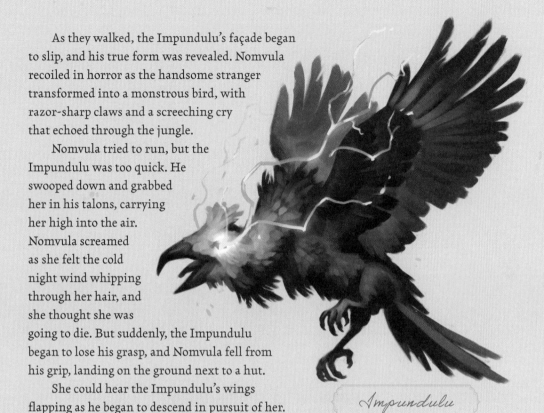

Impundulu

GROOTSLANG

A MISTAKE MADE BY THE GODS

FREAKY FACTS

LOCATION: SOUTH AFRICA

FIRST WRITTEN MENTION: 1274

CLASSIFICATION: SERPENT-ELEPHANT HYBRID

PERSONALITY: FORMIDABLE, MYSTERIOUS, DANGEROUS, AND MALEVOLENT

In the Khoikhoi and San cultures of the western half of South Africa, there is a monstrous legend of a creature that was considered a mistake by the gods who created it. This creature is known as the Grootslang. According to the myth, the Grootslang was the first creature created by the gods, but due to their inexperience, they bestowed it with excessive intelligence and strength.

Realizing their error, the gods attempted to rectify it by dividing the Grootslang into two separate species: one resembling a snake and the other resembling an elephant. However, a few Grootslangs managed to escape and found refuge in the dark caverns of the earth, where they multiplied and assumed the role of treasure guardians.

The name Grootslang translates to "big snake" in Dutch and Afrikaans, which reflects its appearance. Described as a massive serpent with features reminiscent of an elephant, the Grootslang is a fearsome creature.

One of the most renowned lairs of the Grootslang is the Wonder Hole or Bottomless Pit cave located in Richtersveld, South Africa. This cave has attracted numerous explorers and treasure seekers who believe it to be brimming with precious jewels and stones, with connections to the sea and other bodies of water. However, entering the cave poses a grave risk, as one may incur the wrath of the Grootslang, which has the power to crush intruders with its coils or devour them whole.

The only treasure that is worth dying for is someone you love. But if you risk that person's life for riches, then you may deserve to be devoured by the treasure's monstrous, slithering keeper.

The legendary Bottomless Pit cave, located in the heart of modern-day Richtersveld, South Africa, was shrouded in mystery. The tales of hidden treasure and the ancient creature said to guard it captivated Mark and his girlfriend, Sarah. They yearned for excitement and sought to test their courage by embarking on a perilous journey into the depths of the cave.

Equipped with flashlights, ropes, and backpacks filled with provisions, Mark and Sarah set off for the cave. The anticipation of what lay ahead was mingled with a tinge of fear, but their youthful exuberance overshadowed any reservations. They believed the legends were just stories made up by, in their minds, superstitious natives.

As they descended into the gaping jaws of the cave, the darkness enveloped them, and the air turned cold and damp. The walls seemed to breathe with a life of their own, and strange shadows danced on the stone. Mark and Sarah's excitement gave way to apprehension, but they reassured each other that the expedition would be worth it once they discovered the rumored treasure.

Deeper and deeper they ventured, the narrow passageways twisting and turning, leading them further into the belly of the Earth. Strange sounds echoed through the cave, eerie whispers that made their skin crawl. Yet they pressed on, drawn by an irresistible urge to find the treasure.

The deeper they delved, the more the cave seemed to come alive with ancient secrets and forgotten nightmares. Sarah clung to Mark's arm, her heart pounding in her chest as tales of the Grootslang, a giant cave-dwelling snake, played in her mind like a haunting melody. But Mark, ever the thrill-seeker, couldn't resist the allure of the unknown.

Finally, they reached an enormous chamber, its walls gleaming with mysterious gemstones that sparkled in the dim light. The sight was breathtaking, and the temptation to fill their bags with precious jewels was almost overwhelming. But they hesitated, remembering the warnings about the creature that supposedly guarded this treasure trove—the horrible Grootslang.

As they debated whether to proceed, a low rumble echoed through the cave, shaking the ground beneath their feet. A cold chill swept over them, and they knew immediately that they had awoken something ancient and powerful.

"We should leave, Mark. This is too dangerous," Sarah pleaded, her voice trembling.

But Mark's greed got the better of him. He convinced himself that the Grootslang was merely a myth, a legend meant to keep others away from the treasure. Ignoring Sarah's pleas, he began filling his bag with gemstones.

Suddenly, the ground shook violently, and the chamber seemed to close in on them. The Grootslang emerged from the darkness, its immense form casting a shadow over the treasure-laden cave. It resembled a colossal serpent with the head of an elephant, its eyes gleaming with an ancient intelligence.

Sarah's fear turned to terror as the Grootslang's massive coils encircled Mark, squeezing the air from his lungs. He dropped the bag of jewels, gasping for breath as he struggled against the creature's deadly embrace.

"Please, let him go! We didn't mean to disturb you," Sarah cried, her voice desperate.

But the Grootslang's intelligence seemed to understand neither reason nor plea. It tightened its grip, and Mark's pleas for mercy grew weaker until they were silenced altogether. The creature devoured him whole, and the cave fell silent once more, save for Sarah's sobs.

The Grootslang regarded her with its ancient eyes, but, terrified and broken, Sarah ran for her life, vowing never to return to the Bottomless Pit cave.

GHOUL

THE DEMONIC CANNIBAL THAT DWELLS IN GRAVEYARDS

FREAKY FACTS

LOCATION: WEST AFRICA

FIRST SIGHTING: 610–632

CLASSIFICATION: HUMANOID DEMON

PERSONALITY: CANNIBALISTIC, SCAVENGER, STEALTH, AND MALEVOLENT

Out of the northern part of the continent of Africa comes an evil undead creature from Arab legend: the Ghoul. This devilish creature has been a part of Arab beliefs since before the advent of Islam. The noun "ghoul" and its related adjective "ghoulish" are sometimes used interchangeably to refer to many demons, monsters, or ghosts. However, the term actually refers to a specific creature.

Throughout various historical times, the Ghoul was described as an ugly, humanlike monster who inhabited the desert and desolate regions, where it would lie in wait for travelers. It would trick them by lighting a fire and leading them off their path. Once they were lost, the Ghoul would attack, kill, and devour its prey.

The Ghoul is also said to dwell in graveyards and cemeteries, where it may rob graves and feast upon corpses. Ghouls drink the blood and eat the flesh of their victims, whether living or dead. Once it consumes a meal of human flesh, it is said to have the ability to take on the person's form. This isn't its only supposed ability to shapeshift; it can also assume the form of animals, usually the hyena.

In some versions of the legend, if a person drinks the blood of a Ghoul, they will turn into one. But ironically, in another version, to remain young, strong, and heal quickly, one must consume Ghoul blood once a month—not an appetizing routine.

Ghouls are quick and strong, making them hard to beat, but there are ways to defend yourself against them. They are said to be afraid of church bells, and because they aren't very intelligent, they are easy to trick.

It is bad luck to stand on someone's grave, so why would anyone even think about playing in a graveyard? The dead aren't the only ones who call the graveyard home—Ghouls do as well.

Tiny wisps of clouds cast ominous shadows across the graveyard in a small village in Morocco as Ahsan darted between headstones, looking for a place to hide. His brother Abdul was counting and had almost reached the agreed number before yelling, "Ready or not!" Ducking behind a large, crumbling mausoleum, Ahsan could hear his brother's footsteps as he began his search.

He covered his mouth to stifle a giggle when his brother passed him by for the second time, unaware that he was so close. Ahsan had been so focused on his brother's calls and footsteps that he hadn't noticed the breakage in the stone structure he was leaning against, so he let out a frightened yelp when he fell through the wall and landed on his back next to a dusty old coffin.

He was trying to examine a nasty cut on the back of his leg when he heard something scuttling around in the dark tomb behind him. Ahsan's heart pounded in his chest as he turned to face the source of the noise. With wide eyes, he caught a glimpse of a pair of glowing red orbs in the darkness. Fear gripped him, and he froze in place, unable to move or even scream for help.

"Wh-who's there?" Ahsan stammered, his voice trembling.

In response, a low, guttural growl emanated from the shadows, sending Ahsan's heart into a panicked frenzy. He tried to scramble backward, but his legs felt weak and uncooperative. The growling grew louder, and the red eyes drew closer. Ahsan's mind raced, trying to make sense of what was happening. Was this some kind of animal? Or was it something else entirely?

Suddenly, the creature emerged from the darkness, revealing a hunched, emaciated figure with sharp claws and jagged teeth. Its skin was a sickly gray color, and it was covered in grime and dried blood. Ahsan's eyes widened in terror as he realized what he was looking at: a Ghoul.

The Ghoul hissed, its unnaturally long tongue flickering out between its sharp teeth. Ahsan's heart pounded in his chest as he tried to back away, but his body refused to cooperate. Fear had paralyzed him, leaving him at the mercy of the evil creature before him.

The Ghoul took a step closer, and Ahsan could feel its foul breath on his face.

"P-please, don't hurt me," he pleaded, his voice barely above a whisper.

The Ghoul's eyes seemed to bore into Ahsan's soul, and for a moment he thought he saw a glimmer of something almost human in its gaze. But the moment passed, and the creature lunged, its claws reaching for Ahsan's throat.

In a desperate attempt to defend himself, Ahsan raised his hands to shield his face, but it was futile. The Ghoul's claws tore through his flesh, and he let out a scream of agony. The pain was overwhelming and he could feel his strength fading fast.

As darkness closed in around him, Ahsan's mind flashed back to his family and his village. He thought of his brother Abdul, who would be worried when he couldn't find him. He wished he could see his family one last time, to tell them how much he loved them.

But that wish would never come true. The Ghoul's relentless attack had taken its toll, and Ahsan's life slipped away, leaving his body lying lifeless on the cold tomb floor.

On the other side of the graveyard, Abdul grew worried when, after over an hour, he couldn't find his little brother, Ahsan. He ran back to the village to get help and returned with several of their friends. They searched frantically, calling out his name as they combed the graveyard. And then Abdul found him—still and motionless—beside the dusty old coffin. His body had bites taken from it.

Abdul fell to his knees, tears streaming down his face, as he cradled his brother's lifeless body in his arms. But then he heard something scuttling around in the tomb behind him. Abdul's heart pounded in his chest as he turned to face the source of the noise. With wide eyes, he caught a glimpse of a pair of glowing red orbs in the darkness.

ghoul

AUSTRALIA AND NEW ZEALAND

Australia is known for having some of the world's most dangerous animals. You may have heard it said that "everything in Australia can kill you," but it's not just real-life creatures you need to be on the lookout for. There are numerous mythical Australian creatures that live in the bush and stalk the outskirts of major cities too. Australian folklore is steeped in the eerie and enigmatic with stories of malevolent creatures lurking in remote waterways, and tales of hairy beasts that roam the wilds, reminding you that danger isn't just confined to the natural world.

New Zealand's folklore is a realm where ancient entities cast a shadow over breathtaking landscapes and reveal the spine-tingling depths of Māori mythology, adding a truly otherworldly dimension to the country's allure.

YARA-MA-YHA-WHO

THE FROG-LIKE AUSTRALIAN VAMPIRE THAT HANGS AROUND IN FIG TREES

FREAKY FACTS

LOCATION: NORTHERN AUSTRALIA

FIRST SIGHTING: PREDATES WRITTEN HISTORY

CLASSIFICATION: VAMPIRIC FROG CREATURE

PERSONALITY: DECEPTIVE, CUNNING, UNSETTLING, BLOODTHIRSTY, AND MALEVOLENT

The Yara-ma-yha-who is depicted as a short, stout creature with a toad-like appearance. It sports vibrant red fur and a bulbous nose that aids in tracking its prey. Lacking teeth, it feeds using the jagged suckers on its hands and feet, tearing through flesh to consume blood.

Within the Australian Outback, entire Yara-ma-yha-who colonies inhabit fig trees, patiently awaiting unsuspecting travelers to wander into the shade. As the victims seek respite from the scorching heat, the creatures emerge from the branches, rend their flesh, and indulge in their blood.

The Yara-ma-yha-who deliberately leaves sufficient blood in its victims' bodies, ensuring they stay alive while the sadistic creature satisfies its appetite. Some attribute this behavior to their queen. Once hunger strikes, the queen positions herself before the victim, crawling lizard-like, mouth agape, and engulfs the victim headfirst. Afterward, she stands and proceeds to dance around until the meal is fully consumed.

Subsequently, the Yara-ma-yha-who queen then ventures to a nearby river, lake, or pond, drinking a substantial amount of water before dozing off. Upon awakening, she regurgitates the remnants of her recent feast. She prods and tickles the victim to ensure they are not feigning death. If the victim remains motionless and silent, she returns to slumber, granting them an opportunity to escape.

A Yara-ma-yha-who never passes up the chance to attack the same victim repeatedly, causing them to shrink in size, become redder, and increasingly crave blood with each assault. The exact number of attacks required remains unknown, but anyone foolish enough to continue dozing under fig trees will eventually transform into a Yara-ma-yha-who themselves.

Vampiric creatures come in all shapes and sizes, but these Australian bloodthirsty predators are horrifyingly unique, and they never dine alone. Poachers are predators as well, so if one becomes a meal for the Yara-ma-yha-who, will he really be missed?

One hot summer day a middle-aged poacher named Jack ventured into the Australian outback to pursue his illegal trade. He set traps and snares to capture elusive creatures for profit.

It was a scorching day as the relentless sun beat down upon Jack while he trudged through the parched landscape. His skin glistened with sweat and thirst gnawed at him, but he pressed on, driven by the promise of a hefty payday.

Yara-ma-yha-who

As the day wore on, the heat became unbearable, and Jack's body begged for rest. Seeking shelter, he stumbled upon a grove of fig trees, their green canopy providing a tantalizing escape from the sun's harsh rays. Unaware of the malevolent presence hidden within the branches, he sought refuge beneath the welcoming shade.

As Jack leaned against a tree, the air seemed to shift, and an ominous silence descended upon the grove. Unbeknownst to him, a colony of dangerous creatures lurked above, their red fur blending seamlessly with the figs' foliage.

Suddenly, the branches trembled, and the creatures emerged, their bulbous noses sniffing the air for potential prey. Jack's heart quickened as he realized he was not alone. He attempted to flee, but it was too late—the Yara-ma-yha-who descended upon him with lightning speed, their sucker-like appendages latching onto his skin.

Pain shot through Jack's body as the creatures tore through his flesh, draining his blood with grotesque efficiency. Paralyzed with terror, he could do nothing but watch in horror as the creatures feasted upon his life force.

The Yara-ma-yha-who deliberately left him alive, ensuring he remained conscious and aware of his nightmarish fate. In the distance, Jack caught a glimpse of what must be the queen—a creature larger and more sinister than the others. She crawled toward him like a lizard, her mouth agape, preparing to consume him headfirst.

As she began her gruesome feast, Jack's vision blurred, and he felt himself growing weaker with each passing moment. The pain was unbearable, and he knew he may not survive. Desperation gripped him, and he fought to stay conscious, praying for a chance to escape.

He became trapped inside the belly of the queen, and those few minutes felt like hours while she napped. Then, suddenly, the walls of her stomach began to constrict violently, until with a *whoosh* she spewed him out.

With a surge of adrenaline, Jack mustered every ounce of strength he had left. When the queen prodded and tickled him, he forced himself to remain motionless and silent, masking his pain as best he could. Incredibly, the queen believed he was already dead and returned to her slumber, granting him a fleeting opportunity to escape.

Summoning his last reserves of energy, Jack stumbled away from the fig grove, his body weakened and covered in bite marks. He knew he couldn't rest until he was far away from the Yara-ma-yha-who's cursed territory. As he hobbled through the outback, he felt a burning sensation in his veins—a craving for blood.

Unbeknownst to Jack, he had become tainted by the Yara-ma-yha-who's malevolence. With each passing day, he felt himself growing smaller, his skin redder, and his thirst for blood insatiable.

BUNYIP

THE LEGENDARY, SMELLY WATER MONSTER OF AUSTRALIA

FREAKY FACTS

LOCATION: NORTHWESTERN VICTORIA AND NEW SOUTH WALES, AUSTRALIA

FIRST SIGHTING: PREDATES WRITTEN HISTORY

CLASSIFICATION: WATER MONSTER

PERSONALITY: MYSTERIOUS, ELUSIVE, AND MALEVOLENT

Stories originating from the Wemba Wemba people of northwestern Victoria and southwestern New South Wales tell of the Bunyip, a creature rumored to dwell in billabongs, swamps, and rivers that has been the subject of numerous reported sightings over the years.

The most prevalent depiction of the Bunyip is that of a wretched and foul-smelling creature lying in wait for unsuspecting prey to pass by before launching its attack. Descriptions list a long neck, a rounded head, and a body resembling that of a hippopotamus or manatee. The Bunyip is also said to emit "roaring noises" before devouring its meal. Unsurprisingly, the preferred prey of the Bunyip is said to be young children and women. The term "Bunyip" roughly translates to "demon" or "devil" from the Wemba Wemba language.

During the 1840s and 1850s, as European settlers expanded their territories, numerous Bunyip sightings were reported, particularly in the southeastern colonies of Victoria, New South Wales, and South Australia. One notable account comes from an English convict named William Buckley, who had escaped from a penal colony near modern-day Melbourne and lived among the First Nations peoples. Buckley described the Bunyip as an "extraordinary amphibious animal" covered in gray feathers and claimed to have witnessed it killing and consuming a woman from his adopted village.

Australia, one of the largest countries on Earth, is the only one that covers an entire continent. There, you will find unlimited places to get into trouble. If you are looking for adventure: Australia. If you are looking for danger: Australia. If you are looking for monsters . . . Australia.

An adventure-seeking young man by the name of Shibby had traveled to Australia after college, hoping to experience the truly exciting "Outback." He quickly landed a job on a ranch working for the Johnston family. The other ranch hands made sure to tell him about every terrifying creature, real and made-up, that they could think of. Scaring the new guy was always great fun. Soon, though, Shibby would get more excitement than he had ever imagined.

It all happened late one night. Shibby and Mr. Johnston had decided to camp out near the billabong where they had found a dead mickey bull earlier in the day. They wanted to kill the creature behind the mysterious deaths that had been happening on the ranch. As

WHOWIE

The Whowie, a feared creature known to inhabit the Riverina region, has its main residence in a cave on the banks of the River Murray. This formidable creature measures approximately 20 feet (6 m) in length and bears a resemblance to a goanna, albeit much larger in size. Notably, it possesses six legs on each side of its body and boasts an elongated tail. Its build is reminiscent of a frog, complete with a massive head.

With its cunning nature, the Whowie is known to pounce on and consume anything that crosses its path. It possesses the ability to stealthily infiltrate unguarded camps, devouring one or two victims and carrying the rest, too large to be swallowed, back to its lair within its mouth. The Whowie's movements are deliberate and unhurried, emphasizing its methodical nature.

they huddled around the campfire, the air was heavy with tension, and an eerie silence enveloped the area.

Suddenly, a low, guttural growl echoed through the darkness, freezing them in their tracks. Mr. Johnston gripped his rifle tightly, his weathered face etched with concern.

"What was that?" Shibby whispered, his voice trembling.

Mr. Johnston's eyes darted around, scanning the shadows for any sign of movement. "I'm not sure, but we better stay alert. There's definitely something out there," he replied in a hushed tone.

As the night wore on, the tension in the air thickened, and a sense of foreboding settled over them. Shibby's mind raced with thoughts of the Bunyip—the terrifying creature rumored to lurk in the billabongs. It was one of the scariest creatures that the other guys had warned him about, but he had dismissed the stories as mere banter. But now, faced with the unknown, he couldn't shake the feeling that there was some terrifying creature out there, waiting to attack.

Bunyip

Then, they heard it—the unmistakable sound of heavy footsteps approaching their camp. Shibby's heart leaped into his throat as he clutched the handle of his shovel, the only weapon he had at hand.

Out of the darkness emerged a grotesque figure. Its long neck swayed side to side, its rounded head adorned with twisted horns. Its body resembled that of a monstrous manatee, and the stench of decay emanated from its wretched form.

Shibby and Mr. Johnston stood frozen in fear as the creature fixed its gaze on them. Its eyes glowed with an otherworldly intensity, and its gaping maw revealed rows of jagged teeth. Its booming roar echoed through the night, chilling them to the bone.

In that moment, Shibby realized that the Bunyip was no mere myth—it was very real, and they were in grave danger. He could feel its malevolence emanating from its very

AUSTRALIA AND NEW ZEALAND
—

being, and he knew that they were mere moments away from becoming its next meal.

"Stay calm," Mr. Johnston whispered, his voice shaking. "We need to slowly back away and make a run for it."

But before they could make a move, the Bunyip lunged forward with lightning speed. Shibby's instincts kicked in, and he swung his shovel with all his might, striking the creature in the side. The Bunyip let out a deafening screech, its bloodshot eyes burning with rage.

Their campfire cast flickering shadows on the ground, and Shibby could see the Bunyip advancing, its massive form towering over them. Panic surged through him, but he refused to back down. He knew they had to fight for their lives.

Mr. Johnston fired his rifle, the sound echoing through the night. The Bunyip roared in pain, but it didn't retreat. It seemed unfazed by their feeble attempts to defend themselves.

Desperation filled Shibby's heart as he realized their chances of survival were slim. With each passing moment, the Bunyip seemed to grow more aggressive, its hunger for their flesh insatiable.

Just as hope seemed lost, a distant sound pierced the night—a pack of wild dingoes howling in the distance. The Bunyip's ears twitched, and its attention shifted momentarily. Sensing an opportunity, Shibby and Mr. Johnston seized their chance and sprinted toward safety, the terrifying roars of the Bunyip fading behind them.

They ran as if their lives depended on it, not daring to look back until they had put a considerable distance between themselves and the billabong. Breathless and shaken, they collapsed to the ground, grateful to be alive.

BURRUNJOR

THE CARNIVOROUS AND MYSTERIOUS DINOSAUR CRYPTID FROM NORTHERN AUSTRALIA

FREAKY FACTS

LOCATION: NORTHERN AUSTRALIA

FIRST SIGHTING: 1957 (BUT THE STORIES PREDATE WRITTEN HISTORY)

CLASSIFICATION: CRYPTID DINOSAUR

PERSONALITY: RECLUSIVE, PREDATORY, ELUSIVE, AND MYSTERIOUS

Have you ever wondered why most of Australia's legendary folklore creatures are also cryptids? Perhaps it's because it's easier to believe in monsters in Australia than anywhere else in the world.

From this region of numerous mysteries, unsettling and unbelievable claims have emerged. These claims date back to Aboriginal folklore and resonate with strange sightings reported by generations of European immigrants, and even occasional tales of close encounters by recent tourists. These tales revolve around a modern-day theropod creature resembling the *Tyrannosaurus rex*.

According to Aboriginal Australian legends, the Burrunjor is a large nocturnal reptile that preys on kangaroos, camels, and cattle. Ancient art depicts a three-toed bipedal creature with small front legs and a large mouth. Locals fearfully avoid specific locations where this creature is said to have been sighted, and they will temporarily leave an area if its footprints are discovered. In eastern regions, the creature is often referred to as "Old Three-Toes" due to the distinct tridactyl prints it leaves behind.

In 1980, there were several reports of mutilated, half-eaten cattle along the Gulf Coast. The stockmen initially thought they were crocodiles, but cattleman Charles Waterman described a "frightsome" 20-foot-tall (6 m), mottled creature with a cow in its mouth that rushed away as he concealed himself behind a bush.

Fellow ranchers pursued the creature, accompanied by their dogs, and when they got to the nearby river, the dogs stopped and began acting strangely. Then, suddenly, the dogs

Otways Panther

OTWAYS PANTHER

Like all cryptids, there is no evidence that the Otways Panther exists, but there have been alleged sightings of this elusive creature scurrying through the Otway Ranges where the bush ends and the beach begins off Victoria's Great Ocean Road.

Since the 1830s, reports of supposed sightings of black panthers in the wild have been recorded. These reports have ranged from rumors among new immigrants about the presence of "big cats" in the wild to sworn testimonies and modern videos. All descriptions have portrayed the mythical beast as a big, black, four-legged animal resembling a panther.

ran away, back toward safety. Something had clearly spooked them. Underneath the men's feet, they discovered unusual "reptilian" tracks, a sight that prompted them to make a hasty departure as well.

Recent sightings of Burrunjor footprints have been frequently reported throughout the Outback. Photographs and casts reveal a consistent bipedal track with three enormous toes, each measuring between 2 and 3 feet (about 1 m) in diameter. These tracks near watering holes, along riverbanks, and even on dirt roads have caused concern among the local populace.

Whether the Burrunjor is real or not, one thing is for certain: There is something mysterious and unsettling lurking in the depths of the Australian wilderness, leaving behind these perplexing tracks. These bewildering footprints continue to fuel the curiosity and fear of those who venture into the vast and untamed Outback.

With so many horrifying monsters dwelling in Australia, sleeping outside doesn't seem like a very wise choice. However, many of Aboriginal heritage still do. Perhaps it's because they see death in a very simple way: as a part of life.

It was dusk as Tjara looked out over the ranch he worked on. He knew every square inch of the land because his ancestors had lived there for many generations.

Tjara had grown up hearing terrifying stories from his elders of a giant reptilian creature that hunted the Outback. He was familiar with the prehistoric rock carvings of the terrifying creature and its three enormous toes. But like many others, he had dismissed these tales as just stories intended to keep children from harm.

Before the recent flurry of sightings and the discovery of the enormous three-toed tracks, that is.

As night fell, Tjara finished his day's work, tending to the cattle and ensuring the ranch was secure. He had been asked by the owner of the ranch to look into the reports of the sightings, but he was uneasy. He had personally observed the reactions of the locals to even the mention of a monster.

Tjara returned to the camp after deciding to heed the warnings. He moved silently through the shadows, his footsteps barely audible on the smooth sand. Only the sporadic rustle of the wind through the dry grass served to break the eerie silence of the Outback.

He stoked the fire inside his modest tent as its sputtering light danced across the walls of the canvas structure. He made an effort to ignore the unsettling sensation that someone—or something—was observing him. He became skeptical due to the old tales. He was a native of the land, however, and was tuned into its rhythms. Tonight, the Outback felt different.

As he lay down to sleep, Tjara's senses remained on high alert. The nocturnal sounds of the Outback surrounded him—the hooting of distant owls, the chirping of crickets, and the occasional howling of dingoes. But in the midst of this natural symphony, there was a startling silence that chilled his bones.

Just when Tjara thought he might drift off to sleep, a low, guttural growl echoed through the night. It was a sound he had never heard before, primal and menacing. The fire crackled louder, causing shadows to dance on the tent's walls, as if trying to mimic the three-toed creature depicted in the ancient paintings.

Tjara's heart pounded in his chest as he tried to convince himself that it was nothing more than a wild animal passing through. But then, the ground beneath his tent trembled, and he felt a faint rumbling sensation.

His mind raced, and he recalled the stories of how the Burrunjor would announce its presence with such rumblings, like a prehistoric beast on the prowl. Fear gripped him, but his pride urged him to face whatever was out there.

With trembling hands, Tjara picked up a makeshift spear, fashioned from a long branch and a sharpened stone. He slowly unzipped the tent, and the dark night greeted him like an abyss of uncertainty.

As he stepped outside, he peered into the darkness, his senses heightened to detect any movement or sound. Suddenly, a powerful gust of wind swept through the camp, extinguishing the fire and plunging everything into darkness.

Now blind in the inky blackness, Tjara's heart raced even faster. He felt vulnerable, like prey caught in the sights of a predator. The eerie silence returned, making him feel as though he had stepped into another realm, a realm where ancient legends came to life.

In that moment of vulnerability, Tjara heard a soft but distinct thud. He froze, his ears straining to catch any further sound. Another thud followed, then another, each one growing louder and closer, causing the earth beneath his feet to quake.

A fear began to wash over Tjara as the moon emerged from behind the clouds, revealing a terrifying sight before him—three enormous, tridactyl footprints imprinted in the sand, each one large enough to engulf him whole.

The Burrunjor was real, and it was here, right in his ancestral land. As the legend was revealed right before him, Tjara could only pray that he had the strength and cunning of his forefathers to face this ancient terror and survive to tell the tale.

Burrunjor

YOWIE

THE SOUTHERN HEMISPHERE'S ANSWER TO BIGFOOT

FREAKY FACTS

LOCATION: NEW SOUTH WALES, QUEENSLAND, WESTERN AUSTRALIA, AND VICTORIA, AUSTRALIA

FIRST SIGHTING: 1875

CLASSIFICATION: HAIRY HUMANOID CRYPTID

PERSONALITY: INTROVERTED AND SHY

Australia's most mysterious cryptid, the Yowie, is thought to be an ancient Aboriginal creature similar to Bigfoot. The Yowie is said to roam the Outback, concealing itself in caves and forests, embodying the legends that have been passed down through centuries and cultural beliefs. This enigmatic creature has left its mark on Australia over time, with physical descriptions that vary in shape and size, often resembling a gorilla.

The Kuku Yalanji peoples from far-north Queensland claim to have coexisted harmoniously with the Yowie for many years, despite alleged instances of the Yowie attacking them.

In 2021, three plantation workers reported that they were on their way home from work when they spotted a figure slouched over under a streetlight. The men claimed to have seen a massive creature covered in dark copper-colored hair, with unusually long arms, and dark skin around its face and chest. It is believed that the creature they saw was the Yowie.

According to accounts, two distinct types of Yowie are believed to exist. One can reach a height of 10 feet (3 m), while the other only reaches 4 or 5 feet (1 or 2 m). They are described as having apelike faces and orangeish-brown hair that can grow to lengths of 2 to 4 inches (5 to 10 cm). Although they are often portrayed as timid, the species is capable of displaying violence and aggression.

Steve Piper, a Yowie hunter, claims to have captured images of what he believes to be this elusive creature on film in 2000. The film has gained significant recognition among fans of cryptids, similar to the 1967 Patterson-Gimlin film from the US, which purports to show Bigfoot (page 15).

Another camping trip goes dreadfully wrong when several friends encounter this terrifying creature in the Australian Outback. It might not have been so bad if it had been the smaller Yowie they had encountered.

The Australian Outback was bathed in the warm rays of the setting sun as Oliver and his friends set up their camp, a satisfying end to a tiring day's hike. They were weary but content, looking forward to a night of rest under the starlit sky. The crackling campfire provided a comforting glow as they exchanged stories and laughter, savoring the brotherliness of their adventure.

As darkness covered the Outback, a rustling in the nearby bushes caught their attention. They dismissed it as a harmless creature, attributing the noise to kangaroos or wallabies that frequented the area. However, their sense of security shattered when a low growl pierced the night, followed by the appearance of an enormous creature before them.

The monstrous being stood at least 8 feet (2 m) tall, its massive frame covered in shaggy hair that seemed to blend with the surrounding darkness. Its long limbs and glowing eyes gave it a nightmarish appearance that sent chills down their spines. Fear gripped their hearts, and panic set in as they realized the peril they were in.

"Run!" Oliver shouted, and they all scrambled to their feet, desperate to escape the terrifying creature. Their hearts pounded in their chests as they sprinted through the bush, the creature hot on their heels. Its thundering footsteps closed in, and terror propelled them forward, seeking some form of sanctuary.

Their desperate flight led them to the edge of a cliff—a dead end. The creature's growls echoed through the night; its eyes locked onto its helpless prey. Fear and hopelessness washed over them as they huddled together, knowing there was nowhere left to run.

The creature approached with an eerie grace, its large form casting a shadow over the petrified group. They could see the hunger in its glowing eyes, the anticipation of its imminent feast. Oliver and his friends clutched each other, preparing for the worst.

Yowie

In the heart-stopping moment before the creature could strike, it halted, its head tilting in curiosity. For a brief, surreal moment, it seemed to observe them with a hint of recognition, as if hesitating despite its bloodthirsty intentions.

"What do we do? What is it waiting for?" whispered one of Oliver's friends, his voice trembling.

Oliver's mind raced for a plan, but he was paralyzed by fear.

Then, without warning, the creature turned around and vanished into the darkness, leaving Oliver and his friends stunned and bewildered. They exchanged confused glances, unable to comprehend the strange turn of events.

As the night wore on, they remained vigilant, afraid the creature might return. The campfire, once a source of comfort, now flickered with an unsettling unease. Sleep eluded them as they recounted the harrowing encounter, unable to shake the feeling that they had come face to face with something otherworldly.

With the first light of dawn, they broke camp, eager to put the horrifying night behind them. They hesitated to speak of the creature, half-afraid that uttering its existence might summon its return. However, as they hiked back, the memory of the creature stayed with them, haunting their thoughts. Was it possible that this creature had just wanted to scare them? Maybe it had a baby nearby, or maybe the Yowie wasn't a monstrous beast after all.

DROP BEAR

THE PREDATORY FANGED KOALA THAT BEGAN AS A PRANK AND BECAME A LEGEND

FREAKY FACTS

LOCATION: ALL OVER AUSTRALIA

FIRST SIGHTING: 1920s–1930s

CLASSIFICATION: URBAN LEGEND (CARNIVOROUS KOALA)

PERSONALITY: MYSTERIOUS, PREDATORY, PRANKISH, AND SNEAKY

A close encounter with the carnivorous and fanged relative of the Australian koala, known as the Drop Bear, is a story that nearly every Australian would recount when asked. For many years, Drop Bears remained undiscovered in the Australian wilderness. However, these days, more and more people are becoming aware of this small Australian predator that hides in tall gum trees.

With shaggy orange fur and dark splotchy patterning similar to most koalas, it is larger than a panther or a large dog. According to descriptions, the creature is a sizable animal, with strong forearms designed for climbing and capturing prey. It bites using broad and powerful premolars instead of canines.

According to legend, Drop Bears can be found in the heavily forested areas of the Great Dividing Range in southeast Australia. Sightings have been reported in the Mount Lofty Ranges, the Southeast, South Australia, and Kangaroo Island. Stories from kill sites and scat analyses indicate that the creature's diet primarily consists of medium to large mammal species, with a preference for larger prey like macropods. Around campfires, people whisper rumors of Drop Bears; bush guides alert unaware tourists; signs are posted by rangers; Australian soldiers are educated to avoid them, and scouts are always prepared. However, what they fail to mention is that the Drop Bear is actually a hoax created to scare tourists. Or is it?

The origin of the Drop Bear myth is untraceable. The first known documented reference in the National Library of Australia can be found in a classified ad from *The Canberra Times* in 1982. However, the word was in common use well before that, particularly to frighten visitors from cities or scouts camping out. If you ever go camping in Australia, it's possible that someone will warn you to watch out for the feared Drop Bear. There will be no chase. You'll be minding your own business when a dark form suddenly drops onto you from above, pinning you down, before you realize that a massive koala is devouring you alive. The locals claim that the only defense is to cover yourself in Vegemite (a popular Australian food spread made from yeast) and adopt an Australian accent.

Imagine encountering a koala that looked like it had taken way too many steroids out in the wilderness of Australia. The cute little bears you have always known as adorable would no longer hold the same place in your heart.

The soft crunch of leaves beneath Ranger Alex's boots broke the silence of the wilderness in the very center of Great Otway National Park, where dense forests and rugged landscapes merge. He was an experienced ranger familiar with the mysteries of the park, but tonight there was a strange air of foreboding.

Drop Bear

As the sun's rays faded away, Alex embarked on his routine patrol. Accompanying him was a young intern named Jake, eager to learn from the experienced ranger. The night held the promise of adventure and discovery, but little did they know that they were about to encounter a horror beyond their wildest imagination.

With their flashlights cutting through the darkness, they ventured deeper into the park. The towering trees loomed like ancient guardians, their branches swaying ominously in the night breeze. Alex sensed that they were being watched, but he dismissed the feeling as a product of his imagination. However, he couldn't shake the feeling that something was amiss.

As they made their way through the forest, a distant cry echoed through the night. "What was that?" Jake whispered, his voice barely audible over the rustling leaves. Alex paused, his senses on high alert. "It's probably just a fox or some other nocturnal creature," he reassured Jake, although uncertainty lingered in his voice.

But deep down, Alex knew that the haunting cry was no ordinary animal. There was an unnatural quality to it, a haunting melody that seemed to seep into their very souls. He urged Jake to stay close as they pressed on, their flashlights guiding their path through the enveloping darkness.

As they approached a clearing, a chilling sight greeted them. The moonlight revealed an ancient tree with gnarled branches that seemed to reach out like skeletal fingers. Beneath it lay a ring of stones, seemingly arranged in some ritualistic pattern.

Alex's heart quickened as he sensed danger emanating from the ancient tree. He had heard rumors of the park being haunted, but he had dismissed them as folklore. Now, faced with the eerie sight before him, he couldn't help but feel that something was off.

"Let's get out of here," Jake said nervously, his eyes darting around the clearing.

Alex agreed, but as they turned to leave, a bone-chilling scream pierced the night. The forest seemed to come alive with a haunting chorus of cries that reverberated through the trees. Panic surged through the two men as they realized they were not alone.

Their flashlights flickered, causing unsettling shadows to dance in the darkness. With a growing sense of urgency, they retraced their steps, desperate to escape whatever evil lurked in the shadows.

But as they ran, a sudden force struck Jake, knocking him to the ground. Alex turned around to find his young companion gasping for breath, his face etched with terror. Across his body sat a huge animal that Alex did not recognize. It had forearms like a gorilla, and its slavering mouth bared rows of jagged teeth. Before he could react, the creature jumped off Jake and grabbed him by the arms. Alex could only watch helplessly as his companion was dragged into the undergrowth, disappearing into the darkness.

Panic and fear consumed Alex as he tried to find his way back to safety. The forest seemed to twist and turn, mocking his attempts to escape. He stumbled through the underbrush, his heart pounding in his chest.

Hours passed, but Alex was trapped in the labyrinth of the haunted park. The cries of unseen creatures echoed in his ears, tormenting him with their unearthly wails. He knew he was no longer alone—the malevolence of the forest had claimed Jake, and now it hungered for him.

As dawn broke, Alex stumbled out of Great Otway National Park, a broken man haunted by the horrors he had witnessed.

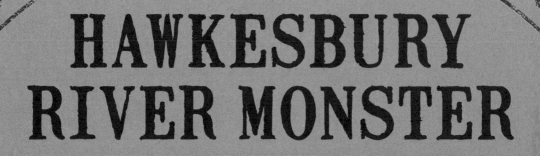

HAWKESBURY RIVER MONSTER

THE AQUATIC CRYPTID OF NEW SOUTH WALES

FREAKY FACTS

LOCATION: HAWKESBURY RIVER, NEW SOUTH WALES

FIRST SIGHTING: 1924

CLASSIFICATION: CRYPTID – REPTILIAN

PERSONALITY: CURIOUS, ELUSIVE, MYSTERIOUS, SHY, AND AGGRESSIVE (OCCASIONALLY)

The Hawkesbury River in New South Wales is the habitat of one of Australia's most peculiar cryptids—the Hawkesbury River Monster. This creature, similar to the Loch Ness Monster of Scotland, is an aquatic lizard species resembling the extinct plesiosaur that existed around 70 million years ago.

According to eyewitness accounts, it measures anywhere between 20 and 70 feet (6 and 21 m) in length. It possesses two pairs of flippers, a long neck, and a head resembling that of a snake. Tales of enormous reptilian or eel-like creatures in the Hawkesbury River date back to at least 1924. In the past decade, reports of this mysterious monster have continued to emerge.

Sightings of the creature have been documented from Wisemans Ferry, in the western part of the river, to the Broken Bay-Brisbane Waters area, at the river's mouth. During the 1980s, a peculiar rumor gained popularity surrounding this creature. Fishermen aboard a small aluminum boat claimed that the sea creature surfaced beneath them, launching the boat more than 10 feet (3 m) into the air and out of the water.

Other accounts include instances of wrecked or capsized boats, as well as boats found adrift with no trace of their occupants.

Sadly, most people who have the incredible opportunity to see a cryptid are ridiculed. People whisper and call them crazy or make them the butt of jokes. Jonah finds out the hard way that if you don't have proof, you might as well not tell.

Jonah was a young fisherman who had grown up in the small fishing village of Juno Point on the banks of the Hawkesbury River. He had heard the tales of the Hawkesbury River Monster since he was a child, but like most of the villagers, he brushed them off as a mere legend meant to scare the young ones.

One dreary afternoon, Jonah set out alone in his rickety boat, hoping for a good catch to help support his family. As he rowed farther into the river, there was a strange feeling nagging at him, but he couldn't quite place it. He glanced around, expecting to see another fishing boat or a curious villager, but there was nothing.

The water seemed unusually calm, almost too still, and the riverbanks were eerily quiet. Jonah tried to focus on his fishing, anxiousness gnawing at him. Just as he was about to give up and head back to shore, he noticed a subtle ripple in the water.

His heart skipped a beat as he saw something massive moving just below the surface.

Jonah's breath caught in his throat as the creature surfaced—an enormous water serpent with a snakelike head, long neck, and large body, flanked by two sets of flippers and an eel-like tail.

Fear paralyzed Jonah as he watched the creature glide through the water, its dark eyes fixated on him. He wanted to turn back, to escape its piercing gaze, but his body seemed frozen in place.

The monster seemed to swim effortlessly, its sleek form weaving through the river's depths. Jonah's mind raced with questions—what was this creature? How had it remained hidden for so long? But as the reality of the situation sank in, his curiosity was quickly replaced by terror.

Suddenly, the creature arched its long neck upward, and Jonah's heart pounded in his chest. The monster stared at him with an intelligence that defied comprehension. It was as if the creature could sense his fear, and that made Jonah's skin crawl.

Desperate to escape, Jonah fumbled with the oars and began rowing frantically back toward the shore. The once-peaceful river now felt like a treacherous trap, and every splash of water made his heart race faster. He dared not look back, fearing that the creature might be following him.

As Jonah's boat neared the riverbank, he felt a surge of relief wash over him. He jumped out of the boat and stumbled onto solid ground, gasping for breath. The monster remained in the water, its presence still lingering in the air.

Jonah's mind was racing, still trying to make sense of what he had just experienced. He looked back at the water, half-expecting the creature to emerge from the depths and attack him. But the water remained still, the monster nowhere to be seen.

Suddenly, Jonah felt a hand on his shoulder. He whirled around, ready to defend himself, but it was just his friend, Sam.

"Are you all right, Jonah? You look like you've seen a ghost," Sam said, concern etched on his face.

"It's . . . it's the monster," Jonah stammered, pointing to the water. "I just saw it, Sam. It's real."

Sam chuckled. "Come on, Jonah, you don't actually believe that old legend, do you? It's just a story."

"No, I swear it's true," Jonah insisted, his voice trembling. "I saw it with my own eyes."

Sam shook his head. "I think you've been out in the sun too long, my friend. Let's get you home and have your mother make you some tea."

MOEHAU

THE BIPEDAL, HAIRY GUARDIAN OF THE LANDS OF NEW ZEALAND

FREAKY FACTS

LOCATION: COROMANDEL PENINSULA, NEW ZEALAND

FIRST SIGHTING: 1969

CLASSIFICATION: CRYPTID – HOMINID

PERSONALITY: CURIOUS, SHY, AND AGGRESSIVE (OCCASIONALLY)

Another terrifying two-legged cryptid may be found on the island of New Zealand. The Moehau is a large, hairy humanoid creature found in the legends of the Māori, the first inhabitants of Aotearoa, the land that later came to be called New Zealand. This mythological creature may be described as a type of Yeti or Bigfoot but with a very aggressive temperament.

MAERO

The Maero is a large, hairy, humanoid creature found in Māori legends. This mythological creature may also be described as a type of Yeti or Bigfoot, but unlike these infamous cryptids, there haven't been any reported sightings of the Maero, even though it does appear to be present in folklore.

It is said that this creature inhabits the rainforests and mountains of New Zealand. In most descriptions, it has a humanlike form but is taller, ranging from 6½ to 8 feet (2 m) tall, more powerful, and has long arms, apelike facial features, and is covered in black hair.

Early encounters often include mention of these creatures acting aggressively and hurling stones to scare off passersby. These monsters, which are mostly found in the Coromandel Range in New Zealand's North Island, are considered to be responsible for the discovery of a prospector's headless, partially eaten body in the Martha Mine area in 1882. Later, a woman's corpse was discovered further up in the foothills. She was found with a broken neck, having been pulled from the shack where she lived while the rest of her family was out.

Photographer and painter Jack Blent claimed to have heard footsteps and trees and twigs breaking in the Ruahine Forest Park in 1963. He had to wait a while before he could see the animal making the noises. It was an enormous, 8-foot-tall (2 m), auburn-colored bipedal ape that was staring at him and murmuring to itself. He ran away in horror.

A 6½-foot-tall (2 m) bipedal ape ran at six campers in 1970 while throwing rocks and yelling as it approached. The campers fled. In the snow-covered peaks of Karangahake, a park ranger discovered many sizable humanlike footprints in 1971.

In 1994, a young girl on her way to a martial arts class in the Bay of Plenty region reported encountering a male Moehau, standing at an impressive height of 8 feet (2 m). Startled by her presence, the Moehau reacted with fear, emitting loud cries and pounding its chest, reminiscent of a gorilla, before hastily retreating on its two legs.

It has been said that the Māori warned early prospectors not to go into the wilderness alone at night. They warned of wild, apelike men that could easily kill warriors. Was this just a story to scare off claim jumpers, or might the Moehau still be out there lurking in the mountains and rainforests of New Zealand?

Living in the country is not for the faint of heart, especially in areas where a legendary cryptid is rumored to live and prey on humans. Always be prepared and never let your guard down. You don't want to be found vulnerable if the Moehau comes knocking.

Just outside of the city of Auckland, New Zealand, in a small country town, a couple decided to leave behind their bustling urban life and purchase a serene farm in the peaceful countryside. Laura and Mark believed it would be an idyllic escape from the city's chaos, a place where they could find peace and tranquility. Little did they know that their quaint farmhouse's location held a terrifying secret.

As they settled into their new home, they adorned their property with bird feeders, relishing the idea of waking up to the sweet melodies of chirping birds. However, their excitement turned to confusion as the bird feeders were mysteriously emptied overnight. At first, they brushed it off as the work of hungry wildlife, but the incidents kept happening.

Soon, strange occurrences became a regularity on the farm. Objects were moved around the property, and heavy items were inexplicably shifted. Their fresh hay bales in the barn were found busted open and scattered across the floor, as if something had rolled around in them. Greasy handprints appeared on their car, almost like a crude warning.

Despite these eerie happenings, Laura and Mark tried to convince themselves that they were simply victims of coincidence. They told each other that it was probably the wind or wild animals causing these disturbances. However, as the nights wore on, they could no longer ignore the chilling knocks and hits on the side of the house. Denial was no longer an option.

One day, Mark had to return to the city for an important business meeting, leaving Laura alone on the isolated farm. What was meant to be a simple day trip turned into an

Mochau

unexpected all-night endeavor. As the sun began to set, the unsettling feeling of being watched crept over Laura. A large apelike creature watched their home from the tree line, and it knew that Laura was alone and vulnerable.

Laura tried to reassure herself that she was safe, but the unnerving knocks on the house intensified, echoing through the night like a haunting symphony. Fear consumed her, and she found herself frantically locking all the doors and windows, desperately seeking solace in the flickering light of her lantern.

The creature's harassment reached a terrifying peak, as if it had been waiting for Mark's absence to claim its prey. It was clear that Laura was what it sought all along. The creature's monstrous presence grew closer, and Laura realized she was not alone. She could hear its guttural growls, its heavy breaths, and its looming footsteps approaching the house.

Fighting back tears, she dialed 1-1-1 and asked for help. The operator said they would send someone out, but the nearest help was kilometers away, and Laura was afraid they wouldn't get there in time.

With the night draped in darkness, the creature's shadow loomed large against the walls of the house. It pounded on the outside walls and doors, its fury now unleashed in full force. Laura was paralyzed with fear, the reality of her vulnerability sinking in.

As the night wore on, the chilling torment continued. When morning finally came, Mark returned to find a constable searching over his property and his farmhouse in disarray, but Laura was nowhere to be found. The creature had claimed its prize, leaving behind only the echoes of its terror.

The tranquil countryside had become a sinister playground for ancient terror, and the city couple's dream of escaping to the country turned into a living nightmare.

MULDJEWANGK

A MAN-FISH HYBRID THAT IS THE PROTECTOR OF THE MURRAY RIVER

FREAKY FACTS

LOCATION: LOWER MURRAY RIVER, SOUTH AUSTRALIA

FIRST SIGHTING: PREDATES RECORDED HISTORY

CLASSIFICATION: CRYPTID – MAN-FISH HYBRID

PERSONALITY: PROTECTIVE, ENIGMATIC, TIMID, CURIOUS, AND AGGRESSIVE (OCCASIONALLY)

There is no known creature scarier than the Muldjewangk according to the Ngarrindjeri people, the Aboriginal Australians who live by the lower Murray River in South Australia and where, they say, the Muldjewangk dwells.

The Muldjewangk is said to be a gigantic half-fish–half-man creature with powerful, oversized hands capable of capsizing ships. A Muldjewangk tale is often shared with young children, although it may seem cruel to inform them of such a terrifying monster. Water creatures, however, have long been utilized as a deterrent to prevent children from straying too close to the water or peering over the sides of boats.

One of the most infamous stories involving the Muldjewangk revolves around a riverboat carrying a substantial number of European passengers. On this particular day, some Aboriginal elders were also aboard the ship. As the tale unfolds, the creature's scaly, clawed hands emerged from the depths of the Murray River, seizing hold of the vessel. Despite his fear, the captain wielded his revolver and began firing. The Aboriginal elders pleaded with him to stop, but the captain persisted. Eventually, the Muldjewangk released its grip on the boat and retreated into the depths.

However, the Muldjewangk's influence on the captain did not end there. It was reported that a few days later, the captain mysteriously fell ill. His body became covered in painful blisters that erupted through his skin. Six months later, he unexpectedly passed away, enduring excruciating pain without any treatment or explanation for his illness.

The land is not the only location where you can encounter a horrifying monster in Australia. Water beasts are just as terrifying and come in large sizes as well.

The Murray River stretched out like a ribbon, winding its way through the dense Australian wilderness. Benjamin, a young lad, eagerly anticipated spending the summer on his family's houseboat. Little did he know that this picturesque river would soon become the setting of a nightmarish encounter he would never forget.

As the days rolled by, the river embraced them with its tranquil beauty, and the nights offered a mesmerizing dance of moonlight on the water's surface. But one particular night, when the moon was at its fullest, everything changed.

Benjamin was lying on the deck, gazing up at the night sky, when he heard something splashing in the water. He stood to look over the edge of the boat expecting to see a turtle or a fish splashing around, but what he saw defied comprehension. At first, he dismissed

Muldjewangk

it as a figment of his imagination, but as the shadow grew larger, his heart began to race with fear. He called out to his mom and dad, who had been relaxing inside the cabin, but they brushed off his concerns as mere childhood fantasies.

Determined to prove the existence of the mysterious shadow, Benjamin grabbed a flashlight and pointed it at the water. His breath caught in his throat when the light revealed a colossal, dark shape moving just beneath the surface. It was no ordinary river creature; it was massive and had an eerie glow about it. The sight caused the hairs on the back of his neck to stand on end, and he rushed into the cabin to alert his family.

FREAKY FOLKLORE
—

His parents, skeptical at first, followed him outside, thinking it might be a school of large fish or some harmless aquatic creature. But their faces turned pale when they too witnessed the ominous presence lurking beneath the boat.

"What is that?!" Benjamin's mother whispered, her voice trembling with fear.

His father's brow furrowed in concern as he tried to identify the creature. "I've never seen anything like it before. We should probably get out of here, now!"

But before they could make a move, the water around them churned violently, and the creature emerged, revealing its monstrous form. It had glowing eyes, long tentacle-like appendages, and a gaping mouth with rows of sharp teeth. Benjamin's heart pounded like a drum, and he clung tightly to his parents as the boat rocked violently from side to side.

The creature was fierce, slamming its massive body against the boat, trying to capsize it. Fear filled the cabin as Benjamin and his parents huddled close to one another. The boat creaked and groaned under the immense pressure, and the family knew their lives were in danger.

Hours passed like an eternity, and the relentless assault of the creature showed no signs of stopping. Benjamin just knew that at any moment the houseboat would start breaking apart. The creature rested between attacks but never failed to return for the next assault.

Benjamin's dad tried to start the boat, but the engine only made a coughing sound. The monster had damaged it.

The family frantically looked for anything they could use to defend themselves, but they were unequipped to deal with such a powerful monster.

Just as they gave up, a faint glimmer of the rising sun appeared on the horizon. With the first light of dawn, the monster seemed to retreat back into the depths, vanishing as mysteriously as it had appeared. Benjamin, his dad, and his mom hailed help from a passing boat a few hours later. They were eventually towed back to shore, where they immediately put the houseboat up for sale and never returned to the Murray River.

ASIA

Asia is the largest and most populous continent, comprising
forty-eight countries and three other territories. It's no surprise,
then, that Asian folklore is a vast repository of the grotesque and
the fantastical. Demon kings, hopping vampires, and viscera
suckers haunt the forests, temples, and even nightclubs of
the major cities and small towns and villages throughout this
region, while the jinn of old dare you to discover their hiding
places and make a wish.

YUKI-ONNA

THE WINTRY TEMPTRESS WITH ICY BREATH

FREAKY FACTS

LOCATION: JAPAN

FIRST SIGHTING: PREDATES
WRITTEN HISTORY

CLASSIFICATION: YOKAI

PERSONALITY: MYSTERIOUS,
VENGEFUL, COLD, AND
MALEVOLENT

In Japanese legend, *yokai* are ghosts, monsters, or spirits with unique qualities that have the power to evoke a variety of emotions, from fascination to horror. One notable yokai is Yuki-onna, a vengeful spirit often depicted in films, animation, and literature.

The writer Lafcadio Hearn is sometimes credited as having had a significant impact on the spread of Japanese culture in the West. His version of Yuki-onna's tale is perhaps the most well-known.

According to Hearn, the tale of Yuki-onna begins with two woodcutters, Mosaku and his trainee, Minokichi, who lived in a little community in the cold highlands. Every day the two lumberjacks would chop trees in the neighboring forest and bring the lumber back to the village at the end of the day. However, the duo became lost in the forest one day due to a severe snowstorm, so they sought refuge in a dilapidated wood cabin to wait it out. The storm persisted, though, so Minokichi and Mosaku decided to stay there for the night.

Minokichi awoke in the middle of the night to the unsettling sight of a snow-white spirit woman watching over his master. The woman was Yuki-onna. She breathed a blast of icy air upon Mosaku, killing him instantly. She then turned to Minokichi and told him that since he was young and attractive, she would save him from the same fate, but only if he never told anyone what had happened to Mosaku.

For a few years, Minokichi kept his master's death to himself and continued working in the forest. One day, when Minokichi was returning from the woods, he met a gorgeous young woman named Oyuki, and they both felt an instant spark. They became quite close over the next few weeks and became romantically involved. Oyuki eventually moved into Minokichi's family house with him and his mother, where she and Minokichi raised ten children together.

Oyuki was sewing in the dark one night, with only the flickering light of a torch against her face. Minokichi examined her face and began to experience déjà vu.

Her complexion was extraordinarily pale—nearly blue—in the light, and it contrasted sharply with her long, jet-black hair. He'd seen this expression before. He began to tell her about the night his master, Mosaku, was murdered, and then said to Oyuki that she resembled the ghost that killed him.

With an expressionless face, Oyuki slowly turned to Minokichi and said, "Do you not remember what you promised?"

The weather rapidly changed. The stillness gave way to a snowfall. The woodcutter felt an intense shudder run down his spine, and he finally realized who Oyuki was—she was Yuki-onna. She told the woodcutter that if it weren't for their children, she would kill him. Oyuki had Minokichi promise to look after their children, and then she vanished. Minokichi was rendered speechless, and he spent the rest of his days caring for his children. For dread of running into Yuki-onna again, he remained alert and cautious of the woods.

The name Yuki-onna translates to "snow woman" in Japanese. As expected, Yuki-onna is more commonly associated with Japan's hilly regions and the colder seasons, where snow and ice play significant roles in her stories.

KIYOHIME

Kiyohime is renowned for her tale of unrequited love and her transformation into a serpent. According to the story, Kiyohime was deeply in love with Anchin, a Buddhist monk. She relentlessly pursued him to the Dōjō-ji Temple. However, when her affection was rejected by Anchin, she was consumed by rage and transformed into a serpent. In her serpent form, she tracked him down and killed him inside a bell at the temple.

Yuki-onna is described as having exceptionally pale, almost blue skin, representing her cold nature. Some legends even claim that her skin is transparent, allowing her to blend in with the frigid surroundings when she appears on chilly winter days. Her long, jet-black hair frames her alluring face, creating a striking contrast with her skin tone. She is often depicted as taller than average for a woman.

Contrary to popular belief that she wears red kimonos to hide the stains of her victims' blood, Yuki-onna typically dresses in white. Depending on the tale, her age may vary, but most accounts place her in her twenties. She is often described as a stunning young woman who exploits her beauty to deceive people and lead them into her traps.

Yuki-onna is typically portrayed as a malevolent spirit who seeks to harm anyone she encounters. The origins of Yuki-onna vary across different prefectures, but she is commonly believed to have originated from stories of loss and sorrow. Usually, she meets an untimely death by melting or disintegrating into oblivion when exposed to extreme heat.

Only a tragic love story can do justice to the most malevolent Japanese yokai. Many of these entities began with a tragic story of their own, often at the hands of their lover.

Winters were bitterly cold in the remote village hidden deep within Japan's hilly regions. Akira was a young man who lived in this frigidly cold village. He had a reputation for having a good heart. Hana, a stunning local girl with starlike eyes, had become drawn to Akira. As their dreams of a future together bloomed like cherry blossoms in the spring, the two had fallen deeply in love.

Yuki-onna

ASIA

197

But fate can be cruel, and one night, as Akira was returning home from a late visit to Hana's house, he saw a mysterious figure in the distance. It was a woman, draped in white, her jet-black hair cascading like a waterfall down her shoulders. Akira's heart skipped a beat; he had heard enough stories to cause his blood to run as cold as the air around him. Could it be the spirit of the Snow Woman?

His chest was gripped by fear, but he made an effort to reason with himself. Maybe it was just a villager. However, as he got closer, the air grew colder, and he saw the faintest blue tinge on the woman's skin.

Akira's heart pounded as the woman turned her gaze toward him. Her eyes were as cold as the winter night, and a sinister smile crept upon her lips. He tried to run, but his legs felt as heavy as stone, and his body refused to obey his commands.

"Hello, Akira. I am Yuki-onna." She introduced herself and followed with an icy smile.

"I've been watching you, Akira," Yuki-onna whispered, her voice carrying an otherworldly charm. "You are full of warmth and love, a rarity in this frozen world."

He managed to stammer, "W-why are you here?"

Yuki-onna's laughter echoed like icicles breaking. "I have taken a liking to you, Akira. Join me, and you shall never feel the biting chill of winter again."

But Akira's love for Hana burned within him. He mustered his courage and pleaded, "I cannot abandon my life, my love. Please, spare me."

The Snow Woman's smile faded, and her eyes darkened with rage. "Stubborn fool! Your love for that girl will be your downfall."

In an instant, she unleashed her icy breath upon him, freezing the air around him. Akira's body trembled as frost crept over his limbs, turning him into a statue of ice. Yuki-onna's laughter filled the night, and as she vanished into the swirling snow, she left behind only thin shards of floating ice.

The next morning, when the villagers found Akira's frozen, lifeless form, they wept for the loss of the young man's kind soul. Hana, heartbroken, refused to believe that he had simply succumbed to the harsh cold. She knew the legends of Yuki-onna and was determined to avenge her beloved.

As the winter deepened, Hana braved the chilling winds, day after day, seeking the Snow Woman herself. She was willing to risk everything to confront the malevolent spirit and bring justice to her lost love. But one day, she didn't return from her search. It was believed that she had followed Yuki-onna straight to a frozen hell.

JIANGSHI

CHINA'S INFAMOUS HOPPING VAMPIRE

FREAKY FACTS

LOCATION: CHINA

FIRST SIGHTING: QING DYNASTY
(1644–1911)

CLASSIFICATION: VAMPIRIC –
REANIMATED CORPSE

PERSONALITY: MALEVOLENT,
AGGRESSIVE, BLOODTHIRSTY,
STIFF, AWKWARD, AND RESTLESS

For a millennium, undead Jiangshi vampires have hunted, fed on, and infected the living. Unlike Western vampires and zombies, Jiangshi vampires hop—a skill that makes them particularly skilled and potentially terrifying.

Encountering a Jiangshi unexpectedly can be absolutely terrifying, especially if being caught off guard is something you dislike. Jiangshi don't hop randomly: They can appear before or behind you. Similar to Western vampires, Jiangshi were created by the very people who eventually came to fear them, rather than being the work of ancient evil forces.

These hopping vampires originated during Qin Shi Huang's conquest of the Chinese states, over 2,000 years ago. (Qin Shi Huang was the founder of the Qin dynasty and the first emperor of a unified China.) These creatures were believed to have once been living humans. Warriors sent far from home to defend against Qin Shi Huang's forces often perished in battle, leaving their families unable to afford the return of their bodies. Seeking solace and a way to bring back their loved ones, common people sought help from Daoist priests.

To establish a connection with the deceased's body and soul, the priests performed a sacred ritual. By providing specific instructions, they attempted to guide the dead back home. Due to rigor mortis, which stiffens the body, hopping became the encouraged mode of transportation for the returning spirits. Hence, Jiangshi translates to "stiff corpse."

LANGSUIR

Malay folklore brings us an evil female vampire who preys on pregnant women.

Langsuir are women who died as a result of a laboring sickness that killed both mother and child. Because the mother will rise forty days after death, glass beads are placed in the corpse's mouth. The Langsuir is distinct in appearance, having crimson eyes and long, sharp teeth. Their primary victims are pregnant women, whom they murder or in whom they attempt to induce a miscarriage. If no pregnant women are present, the Langsuir will feed on fish.

The Langsuir sucks blood from the victim by means of a hole at the back of the neck. Cutting her claws or covering the opening with the Langsuir's hair will restore her to human form. To survive, they may fly, take the form of an owl, and live in rivers or the sea.

Unfortunately, it is unlikely that any of the original Jiangshi successfully reunited with their families. Grieving families, instead of losing faith in the local priests, believed that something had gone wrong during the ritual. They saw their departed family members as reanimated beings, lacking the goodness of their souls.

Unlike the vampires of Eastern Europe, Jiangshi couldn't leave their graves. They were the result of negligence, and one can only speculate on the number of corpses left in the wake of Qin Shi Huang's wars that covered the early Chinese roads and fields.

These poor souls left unburied transformed into Jiangshi during the night, achieved through energy absorption. Unburied bodies could reanimate by consuming the vital energy transformed by moonlight or starlight falling upon them.

A hopping vampire, even though he can't fly, is no laughing matter. The creature is still a soulless corpse thirsting for the life force of the living, and it doesn't care who it drinks from. Friend or foe, no one is safe.

In the remote Hemu Village, near the captivating Kanas Nature Reserve of Altay, northern Xinjiang, the simple and ancient lifestyle of the Tuvas, an ethnic group known for grazing animals and hunting, flourished. The village's breathtaking beauty drew visitors from far and wide, especially during the enchanting autumn season.

One fateful day, tragedy struck Hemu Village when a loaded tour bus lost control on the winding hills and rolled down the hillside, claiming the lives of several passengers. Among the wreckage, rescuers made a gruesome discovery—the crushed body of a young local farmer who had recently married his childhood love.

Overwhelmed by grief, the widow of the farmer resorted to desperate measures to bring him back to life. Rumors circulated that she had summoned a Daoist priest, renowned for performing rituals to resurrect the dead. The widow secluded herself, shutting out the world, and kept her deceased husband's body within the confines of her home.

After several weeks, the village became shrouded in an eerie atmosphere. Mirrors were covered, and the villagers felt a sense of impending doom as strange incidents occurred, including the unexplained disappearance of a tourist and the mysterious death of a young schoolgirl.

Amidst this unsettling atmosphere, Chen, a young boy who had grown up in Hemu Village, walked to the river by the forest with his friend Jian for a leisurely afternoon of fishing. As they roamed the serene landscape, the day took a dark turn when Chen's dad's prize milk cow vanished from the barn. Chen was summoned home to help search for the missing cow. Following the sound of a distant cowbell, Chen ventured deep into the forest, where an encounter with a nightmarish figure unfolded.

Without warning, something dark swooped down out of the sky and grazed the top of his head. With a sharp scream, Chen let go of the limb of a nearby tree he had been holding for balance, but the limb bounced back and smacked him in the face, knocking him to the ground.

Stunned, he lay there with the cold earth beneath him. He felt something warm running down his cheek; it tickled. He reached up to rub it away, but when he pulled his hand back, there was blood on his fingers. The branch had made a purchase and left a nice little cut.

Frustrated and tired, Chen climbed back to his feet, but he froze when he heard another thump, closer and heavier than before. He stood there, waiting and listening, and again, there was another thump and crackling of limbs. The sound seemed to be coming from behind him.

Chen slowly turned around, trying to be as quiet as possible so as not to give away his position, as if his fall just now hadn't already done that.

Not far away, in a small opening in the forest where the moonlight was beginning to shine down, he could see a figure. It was just standing there about 20 feet (6 m) away from him with its face hidden in the shadow of an overhanging tree branch.

All of a sudden, with a heavy thump, the creature materialized before him a mere 10 feet (3 m) away. He could now make out the details of its appearance. It was a man with a very familiar face, but it was not a normal face.

The skin was saggy, the eyes were clouded with a white haze, and the skin and hair were white with a slight green tint. The creature had both arms outstretched toward Chen, baring long black fingernails.

While Chen stood there trying to understand what and who he was looking at, the creature opened its mouth and, slowly, a grotesquely long tongue began to slide out. It was dripping with thick saliva or some other thick, disgusting ooze.

Chen was almost knocked over with the force of the overpowering smell of decay. He fought the urge to gag.

At the point when Chen's fear was just about to take control, the creature lunged again. Before it could land and sink its claws into his flesh, a burst of adrenaline took over, and Chen turned and began to run for his life.

Chen's heart was pounding fiercely in his chest as he ran as fast as he could through the dense forest. Behind him, he could hear the creature's heavy footsteps and ragged breathing, getting closer and closer with each passing second. He knew he had to keep running, keep moving, or else he would be caught and killed by the monstrous being.

As he ran, Chen cast his mind back to the rumors he had heard about the widow's husband being resurrected by the Daoist priest. Could this creature be the resurrected farmer? Either way, he wasn't going to stick around to find out.

Jiangshi

SHUTEN-DOJI

A JAPANESE DEMON KING WITH A DRUNKEN REPUTATION

FREAKY FACTS

LOCATION: JAPAN

FIRST SIGHTING: SOMEWHERE BETWEEN 794–1185

CLASSIFICATION: ONI

PERSONALITY: CHARISMATIC, CUNNING, DEMONIC, POWERFUL, AND MALEVOLENT

In Japanese legend, Shuten-doji is the fearsome Oni King. An *oni* is a type of yokai or demon in Japanese folklore that's comparable to an Ogre or troll in Western Folklore. Shuten-doji, which translates to "little drunkard" in Japanese, was not always an oni.

His father was the powerful dragon Yamata-no-Orochi, and his mother was a human. There are numerous tales of how he transformed from a boy to a demon, but the most widely accepted one goes something like this: Once, there was a little boy who possessed extraordinary intelligence and inhuman strength. Due to his exceptional abilities, those around him frequently referred to him as a "demon child," which eventually led to the development of a terrible, antisocial personality and resentment toward others.

When he was just six years old, his mother abandoned him. When he was still a child, he became a trainee priest at Kyoto's Mount Hiei. Because he was inherently the smartest and strongest among the young acolytes, he developed resentment toward them as well. This resulted in neglecting his studies and engaging in fights. Furthermore, he began to drink, which violated the monastery's rules, but he could outdrink anyone willing to challenge him. Thus, he acquired the nickname "Shuten-doji," or the "little drunkard," due to his love for alcohol.

One evening, during a festival at the temple, Shuten-doji arrived in a heavily intoxicated state. Throughout the evening, he played pranks on his fellow priests while wearing an oni mask, emerging from the shadows to startle them. However, when he attempted to remove the mask at the end of the night, he found it fused to his face! Ashamed and fearful, he was reprimanded by his masters for being drunk. To avoid interaction with what he perceived as weak, stupid, and hypocritical people, he fled into the mountains. For many years, he lived on the outskirts of Kyoto, stealing food and consuming large quantities of alcohol.

He attracted thieves and criminals, who remained devoted to him, and who formed the core of his gang through his banditry. Eventually, they made their way to Mount Oe, where Shuten-doji plotted to seize the capital and establish Imperial rule from a dark castle. Shuten-doji and his gang abducted noble virgins, draining their blood and consuming their raw organs as they terrorized Kyoto.

A group of heroes led by the legendary warrior Minamoto no Yorimitsu attacked Shuten-doji's palace using a mysterious poison. Even after being decapitated, the intoxicated Shuten-doji's head continued to bite at Minamoto no Yorimitsu. The oni head was buried at the Oinosaka mountain pass outside the city limits, considered impure and belonging to an oni. Rumor has it that Kyoto's Nariai-ji shrine is where Minamoto no Yorimitsu's poison cup and vial are kept.

In the dark corners of Kyoto, where the shadows whisper untold secrets, a group of gullible teenagers attempt to summon the most powerful and evil demon in Japanese folklore. They have no idea that they are like delicate morsels, ripe for the demon to pick.

Deep in the bustling city, hidden away from prying eyes, the group of teenagers closeted themselves in a dimly lit room. They sought the forbidden thrill of summoning the spirit of Shuten-doji. The young and reckless Tomoya led the group, driven by an incessant curiosity and an ability to get into trouble.

With ancient incantations copied from books scrawled on parchment and the pungent aroma of incense filling the air, the group began their ritual. The flickering candlelight cast eerie shadows on their faces as they chanted in unison, calling upon the restless soul of the Oni King.

As the incantations grew louder, the room trembled with an otherworldly energy. Suddenly, the candle flames danced wildly, and a cold wind swept through the chamber. Tomoya's heart pounded in his chest as he felt a malevolent presence lurking nearby.

The teens immediately regretted tampering with the spirit world. In the midst of their fear, a voice echoed through the room, chilling them to the bone. "Who dares disturb my slumber?"

It was Shuten-doji himself, his apparition forming from the darkness. The yokai's face was contorted with rage, and his eyes burned like crimson coals.

The thrill-seekers stood frozen, their minds torn between awe and terror.

Tomoya, ignorant and bold to a fault, spoke to the demon. With trembling hands, he asked, "Shuten-doji, how did you become an oni? What led you down this path of darkness?"

The Oni King's grimace softened into a twisted smile. "Ah, the tale of my transformation is one of sorrow and vengeance." As he recounted his tragic past, the room seemed to grow colder. He spoke of his mother's abandonment, his time at the Mount Hiei monastery, and the cruel fate that bound the oni mask to his face.

The thrill-seekers listened with rapt attention, their fear mixing with a strange fascination. But as the night wore on, the room became suffocating, and a deeply unsettling feeling crept over them.

Shuten-doji

"You have heard my tale," Shuten-doji concluded, his voice growing colder with each passing moment. "Now, it is time for you to join me in eternal servitude."

The group's excitement turned to panic as they realized the gravity of their mistake. Their attempt to harness the power of the Oni King had unleashed a force they could not comprehend.

In a desperate attempt to escape, they scattered, but the little drunkard Shuten-doji had experienced the darkness for far too long. His powers were beyond mortal comprehension, and with a bone-chilling howl he claimed their souls, adding them to his legion of tormented spirits.

KRASUE

THE SEDUCTIVE SPIRIT WHO CRAVES FLESH AND BLOOD

FREAKY FACTS

LOCATION: THAILAND, LAOS, AND CAMBODIA

FIRST SIGHTING: PREDATES WRITTEN HISTORY

CLASSIFICATION: SPIRIT – DISEMBODIED FLOATING HEAD

PERSONALITY: VENGEFUL, GROTESQUE, BLOODTHIRSTY, AND MALEVOLENT

A legendary creature of Thailand, the Krasue is a cursed female spirit that was once a lovely young woman who was burned alive and is now perpetually hungry. The Krasue is also found in other Southeast Asian tales.

The Krasue appears at night as a youthful, attractive woman. The only problem is that this "beautiful woman" wears her internal organs hanging from her neck. She moves by hovering above the Earth with her organs below. The organs usually include a heart, stomach, and digestive system, though sometimes she is depicted with additional internal organs like lungs. The intestines are often shining, speckled with fresh blood. Her teeth are frequently portrayed as vampire-like.

Every night, she goes out in search of blood and flesh. While she appears normal during the day, at sunset her head separates from her body, revealing a truly terrifying sight.

Under the cover of darkness, she is known to attack chickens or cattle, devouring their internal organs and drinking their blood. She might also feed on animal remains, and if fresh blood is not available, she may resort to consuming feces. In the morning, one may discover soiled clothes left outside overnight, supposedly after she wiped her mouth on them.

Due to her insatiable bloodlust, the Krasue also preys on pregnant women in their homes just before or after giving birth. While a woman is in labor, the Krasue hovers around the house, emitting frightful cries that effectively terrorize the mother-to-be. Using a tongue resembling an extended proboscis, she attempts to reach the fetus or placenta inside the womb if she manages to sneak into the house while the mother is unaware or sleeping.

The Krasue is believed to be the cause of numerous diseases that affect pregnant women, particularly in rural areas, as it uses its nasty tongue to catch the unborn child before its birth.

Though it's impossible to verify this malevolent creature's origin story, it is believed that she was once a beautiful young woman who committed many sins that eventually led to her curse.

One story claims that she was a princess who had an adulterous relationship with a soldier. Once her sin was found out, the soldier was beheaded, and the princess was burned to death. Before she died, however, she chanted a spell to protect her body, but the flames engulfed her so quickly that she was only able to save her head and internal organs.

Enter the haunting realm of the Krasue, a malevolent feminine spirit driven by insatiable bloodlust. Will anyone be safe from the clutches of this monstrous apparition with vampire-like teeth, or is it just a matter of time before she claims her next victim?

It promised to be another scorching day on the farm in Kamphaeng Phet, Thailand. Malee began her day as she always did, rising at the rooster's crow of 5 a.m. Though she often hit the snooze button, the actual rooster's chorus compelled her out of bed. Donning her worn-out farm clothes, she ventured out with determination and anticipation. While she tended to the poultry, her husband, Prem, looked after their herd of goats, and they wouldn't reconvene until breakfast a couple of hours later.

However, this day would prove to be unlike any other. Malee discovered her cherished mother goose horribly mutilated. Concerned, she rushed to fetch Prem, only to find him standing over the body of a young goat, subjected to the same dreadful fate as the goose. "What is responsible for this?" she asked him.

His reply was but one word: "Krasue."

The devastation extended beyond the goat and the duck: A dozen of their free-range chickens were also slaughtered, each with their internal organs consumed. Realizing the gravity of the situation, they knew they had to act swiftly. They called on friends and family for assistance, and, with their help, two teams of over fourteen people quickly set to work building fences. These barriers were no ordinary enclosures; they were meant to keep out an ancient creature that had plagued the neighboring villages for generations. The ground was spiked, barbed wire lined the perimeters—it was an intense effort to safeguard their livelihood.

However, amidst the frenzy of construction, Malee began to feel unwell, and she had to return home. The mud smell near the pig pen, which she was accustomed to, suddenly made her nauseous. As she walked home it dawned on her that her monthly cycle was late, and she realized she must be pregnant. Now, they had more at stake than just their animals; something much more precious required protection. Her excitement turned to fear, and she adopted the fierce protectiveness of an expectant mother.

When Prem returned in the evening, she informed him of their new situation. "Prem, we need a fence around the house as well. You're going to be a father, and there's a Krasue out there that will come for our child."

Fatigue weighed heavily on Prem's eyes, but they sparkled with love as he beamed at the news. "I am going to be a father," he echoed.

With determination in his voice, Prem said, "We'll build the fence, and I'll stay up all night to ensure you and our child are safe—every night if I have to."

That night, Prem took the watch to guard against the Krasue, but exhaustion overcame him, and he dozed off. In the darkness, Malee heard a thump and a groan coming from the window, followed by sloshing sounds as something wet slid across the floor. Her heart pounded, and she felt something cold and wet sliding around her neck. Panic set in when she couldn't gasp for air. An agonizing pain burned in her abdomen, just below her ribcage, slowly inching its way down to her belly. Krasue was trying to take her baby, and she was helpless to stop it.

BOOM!

A shot rang out, shattering the silence of the night, and a hint of smoke filled the air. Prem was standing in the doorway, rifle in hand. The Krasue was no match for a father's love.

Krasue

HACHISHAKUSAMA

THE 8-FOOT-TALL WOMAN WHO STEALS CHILDREN

FREAKY FACTS

LOCATION: JAPAN

FIRST SIGHTING: TWENTIETH CENTURY

CLASSIFICATION: URBAN LEGEND – SUPERNATURAL ENTITY

PERSONALITY: TERRIFYING, MYSTERIOUS, ELUSIVE, AND MALEVOLENT

Hachishakusama is a chilling, legendary creature, described as a woman who kidnaps children. Her name translates to "8-foot-tall (2 m) lady" in English. The name is derived from the Japanese words *hachi*, meaning "eight," *shaku*, referring to an ancient measurement unit, and *-sama*, a Japanese honorific that can be translated here to "lady."

In most descriptions, Hachishakusama is portrayed wearing a long white dress and a white *kasa*, an umbrella-like hat. Her long, flowing black hair typically conceals her face. Along with her towering height, she is also depicted with unusually long arms and legs. When she is near, she emits a sound in a masculine voice that goes, *"Po, po, po, po."*

Hachishakusama is often compared to the Japanese version of Slender Man, due to her tall and slender appearance, as well as her chilling obsession with children. According to the legend, she has the ability to disguise herself as the child's relative to deceive them and get close. If she takes a liking to a child, they are doomed and destined to be taken, vanishing forever within a few days.

The fate of the children she takes remains unknown, but it is believed that she feeds off the essence of their souls. One thing is certain: Once she takes a child, they are gone forever.

After Hachishakusama targets a child, that child will forever be in danger. Even if they move away from Japan to avoid her, if they ever return, even as adults, Hachishakusama will be waiting for them.

Although this legend likely originated as a means to scare children into staying close to their parents, it has grown into a story that people of all ages enjoy sharing.

There is a good reason why cautionary tales have been told to children for generations, because kids can be hard to control. It takes monster and ghost stories to keep them safe from their own naïve choices, but sometimes even that isn't enough.

In a small town north of Tokyo lived a curious young girl named Emi who couldn't resist the allure of ghost stories. Each night, she would sneak out of her home to meet her friends at the edge of the woods. There, huddled around a flickering campfire, they would share tales of horror and mystery.

One moonlit night, as the town slept peacefully, Emi's friends recounted the legend of Hachishakusama. They spoke of how she preyed on the innocent and vulnerable, luring them away with her enchanting voice. The mere thought of such a sinister being made Emi shiver, yet she was entranced by the spine-tingling tale.

As the night wore on, Emi's friends dared her to venture deeper into the woods, closer to the abandoned shrine where Hachishakusama was rumored to dwell. With a mix of fear and excitement, Emi accepted the challenge. She felt invincible in the company of her friends, oblivious to the lurking darkness that awaited.

Guided only by the pale moonlight, Emi followed the twisting path that led to the decrepit shrine. The air grew colder, and the rustling of leaves echoed ominously in the distance. With every step, her heart pounded in her chest, but she couldn't back down now—her friends would think she was weak, and the allure of the legend was too strong.

As she reached the shrine, a bone-chilling breeze swept through the trees. Emi's friends urged her to go inside, daring her to face the malevolent spirit. Brimming with false bravado, she pushed open the creaking door and stepped inside.

The interior was filled with an eerie stillness. Broken statues of forgotten deities lined the walls, their once-vibrant colors now faded with time. The oppressive atmosphere suffocated Emi, and her courage wavered. But before she could flee, a haunting melody filled the air, freezing her in place.

PO . . .

PO . . .

PO . . .

PO . . .

The ethereal voice seemed to come from all directions, captivating Emi with its hypnotic allure. Mesmerized, she followed the sound deeper into the shrine. Her friends watched from the outside, their faces etched with concern, but they dared not intervene.

Unbeknownst to Emi, the legend of Hachishakusama was far from a mere tale. The malevolent spirit sensed the young girl's presence and hungered for her innocent soul. With each step, the haunting melody grew louder, drawing Emi closer to her doom.

As Emi reached the heart of the shrine, a figure materialized before her—a tall, spectral woman draped in a blood-stained kimono. Her jet-black hair cascaded down her ghostly face, and her eyes glowed with an otherworldly light. Hachishakusama!

In that terrifying moment, Emi's bravado crumbled, replaced by an overwhelming sense of dread. She tried to turn and run, but an invisible force held her in place, rendering her powerless. The malevolent spirit's unnerving laughter echoed in the chamber.

The other children ran off screaming through the woods and back to town. Their parents woke to the chilling sound of their screams, but by then it was too late. Emi had vanished without a trace, leaving only an eerie silence in the woods.

Hachishakusa-
ma

KUCHISAKE -ONNA

THE VENGEFUL FEMALE SPIRIT WITH AN ETERNAL SMILE

FREAKY FACTS

LOCATION: JAPAN

FIRST SIGHTING: 1970s

CLASSIFICATION: URBAN LEGEND – SUPERNATURAL ENTITY

PERSONALITY: MALEVOLENT, TERRIFYING, MYSTERIOUS, AND ELUSIVE

The ghosts of those who met brutal ends in Japanese folklore find no peace in the afterlife. One such vengeful spirit is known as Kuchisake-onna.

The tale of Kuchisake-onna is macabre, recounting the story of a woman whose mouth was gruesomely split from ear to ear, her spirit returning to seek retribution upon the living. Her name translates to "Slit-Mouthed Woman," derived from the deep, bleeding gash that forms a haunting smile across her face. She materializes at night, targeting individuals who find themselves alone on the streets. To conceal her disfigurement, she wears a cloth mask or employs a fan or handkerchief to hide her hideous mouth.

Under cover of darkness, Kuchisake-onna approaches her unsuspecting victims and poses a question: "*Watashi, kirei?*" ("Am I beautiful?")

If the victim responds affirmatively, she unveils her mask, revealing a grotesque, blood-drenched maw. Softly, she inquires, "*Kore demo?*" ("Even now?"), seeking validation of her attractiveness. Should the victim answer negatively or scream in terror, she mercilessly slashes their face, leaving them with the same mutilated smile. If the victim lies and says "yes" a second time, she departs but trails them home, returning later that night to claim their life.

There is one way that you may possibly escape the clutches of Kuchisake-onna. When she asks you, "Am I beautiful?", tell her that she is average. Or, you can try to distract her with money or hard candies.

The specifics of Kuchisake-onna's past while she was alive remain a subject of debate. Most renditions of the legend portray her as the beautiful mistress or wife of a samurai who suffered from profound loneliness due to his extended absences on the battlefield. Seeking companionship, she engaged in extramarital affairs with men from the town. When news of her infidelity reached the samurai, he was consumed by rage and, as punishment, violently slashed her mouth from the corners to her ears.

There are so many malevolent spirits rumored to dwell in schools, train stations, and even on the streets of the cities in Japan, that it would be terrifying to walk alone at night. But that doesn't stop Ayumi, a fearless young teenage girl from Osaka, until she has a run in with one of these angry spirits.

A chilling breeze swept through the alleys as Ayumi navigated the streets of Osaka, foretelling an encounter that would forever change her life. As the clock struck midnight,

TEKE TEKE

This female ghost from a Japanese urban legend also met a gruesome end, but her demise was the result of a horrific accident. A young woman, or schoolgirl in some versions of the story, tragically fell onto a railway track and was subsequently severed at the waist by an approaching train. She returned as a vengeful spirit known for her unique mode of movement. Using only her hands and elbows, she propels herself forward while dragging her torso, producing a distinct scratching sound: *teke teke*. It is from this sound that she derives her name.

While the spirit is typically depicted as female in the legend, there are instances where Teke Teke is portrayed as a man. Regardless of gender, the spirit possesses extraordinary speed, and if they capture their prey, they will cleave them in half and claim their prey's lower body as their own.

Ayumi found herself wandering down a dimly lit street, her footsteps echoing eerily in the silence. The tall buildings cast long, ominous shadows, creating a haunting atmosphere that caused goosebumps to spread across her skin. Ignoring her unease, she pressed forward, hoping to reach her destination quickly.

Just as she rounded a corner, she saw a figure in the distance. A woman stood there, her face obscured by a mask. She was wearing a long, flowing red dress that seemed to float ethereally around her. Ayumi felt an inexplicable dread deep within her, but her curiosity got the better of her.

"Are you lost, miss?" Ayumi called out with a trembling voice.

The woman turned slowly, and Ayumi noticed that she held a fan in front of her lower face, hiding all but her large, dark eyes. Ayumi guessed by her eyes that she was hiding her beauty behind the mask, but she was wrong.

The woman slowly began to approach, her movements so graceful she seemed to float. Ayumi stood her ground, but that haunting feeling of dread began to grow inside her.

She stopped several feet away from Ayumi and asked in a soft voice, "Do you think I am pretty?"

Ayumi reflexively answered using the manners her parents had taught her. "Yes, you are very pretty."

The woman began to move toward her again with the same grace.

Once the woman was standing directly before Ayumi, she slowly lowered her mask. Ayumi gasped when she saw a truly horrifying sight. The woman's mouth had been sliced on each side from ear to ear. She could see teeth, gums, ligaments, and muscles. The wound looked fresh as crimson blood ran down her jaw.

Ayumi was about to turn and run when the woman reached out and grabbed her upper arm with an iron grip. "Do you think I'm pretty now?" she asked in a soft voice.

Trembling, Ayumi carefully answered, her voice shaking. "Yes, you are pretty."

The iron grip on her arm was released, and the woman began to back away until finally, she disappeared down the dark alleyway.

Ayumi couldn't believe what she had seen. She tried to convince herself it was a mere illusion, a product of her overactive imagination. But the terror she felt that night was all too real and, sadly, it wasn't over.

Later that night, as Ayumi slept, a dark figure wielding a razor floated into her room. Her screams awoke her parents, but it was too late. They found Ayumi lying lifeless on her bed, soaked in blood. Ayumi would now wear a smile for eternity.

Kuchisake-onna

PHI POP

A MALEVOLENT SPIRIT THAT HUNGERS FOR RAW MEAT

FREAKY FACTS

LOCATION: THAILAND

FIRST SIGHTING: PREDATES WRITTEN HISTORY

CLASSIFICATION: SPIRIT – GHOST

PERSONALITY: VENGEFUL AND MALEVOLENT

Another malevolent entity that comes from the folklore of Thailand and that craves human viscera is the Phi Pop. This ghost possesses the ability to enter a human host and feed on its internal organs, refusing to depart until the host's demise. The ghost conceals itself within the host, inducing an insatiable desire for raw meat.

The Phi Pop was once a person of immense power or sorcery. After the person did something forbidden, the black magic backfired, and they became a cannibalistic ghost. Even today, Phi Pop spirits are blamed for mysterious deaths in rural Thailand and Laos.

One popular Phi Pop legend tells of a prince who discovered a mystical method of inhabiting another living being's body. Unbeknownst to him, his servant overheard the incantation and replicated the words, thereby entering the prince's body. Consequently, the prince found himself trapped, unable to return to his original form. In a bid to inform his wife of the situation, he occupied the body of a bird and flew to her.

Swiftly, the wife ordered the servant's body to be destroyed and challenged him to enter the body of an animal. Unaware that his former body had been eradicated, the servant became ensnared within the animal, while the prince was able to reclaim his own body. Since then, the servant has been compelled to transfer from one body to another, consuming the organs of each host.

Phi Pops are formidable specters, capable of devouring a person's intestines while they slumber after successfully possessing them. One method of dispelling this malevolent ghost involves enlisting the services of a spirit doctor, who employs a spirit dancer to drive it away. As the patient watches the dancer's movements, the Phi Pop is drawn into the spinning motion and extracted from the body.

An encounter with a malevolent entity can end in a variety of ways. Those endings aren't always happy. But if you are fortunate enough to survive, there is no doubt that you will be forever changed.

In the busy city of Bangkok, Thailand, Niran, a young accountant, was struggling as his life had taken a dark turn. Grappling with financial woes, he sought solace in the chaos of the city's nightlife, drowning his worries in alcohol and gambling. On one fateful evening, as the neon lights danced around him, Niran found himself in a dingy bar, desperate for a stroke of luck.

Amidst the smoky haze, Niran's eyes met those of a pale and sickly man sitting in a dimly lit corner. He wasn't sure why, but he felt drawn to the man as if he was beckoned by him. Something about the man's gaze sent a shiver down his spine, but the allure of a potential solution to his problems drew Niran closer. He approached the man cautiously, hoping for a way out of his hardships.

As Niran stood before the stranger, the man's cold, bony hand gripped his shoulder tightly. A sudden wave of dizziness washed over Niran, and his surroundings seemed to blur. In that moment, something changed inside him, but he couldn't put his finger on what had transpired.

The stranger's grip loosened, and he collapsed onto the floor, lifeless. Panic surged through Niran as he tried to comprehend what had just happened. The bar patrons rushed to the man's side, but it was too late. The sickly man was dead.

Unbeknownst to Niran, an ancient malevolence had been lurking within the stranger, seeking a new host to continue its grisly existence. The Phi Pop, a malevolent entity that fed on human intestines while its host slept, had now found a new vessel—Niran.

Days passed, and Niran's life took a sinister turn. He experienced night terrors, waking up in cold sweats with vivid images of a grotesque figure lurking in the shadows. Each morning, he felt weaker and more fatigued, unable to comprehend the changes consuming him.

Driven by desperation and a gnawing fear, Niran sought answers from the city's spiritual underworld. It was there he learned about the Phi Pop, an entity that moved from one host to another, leaving behind a trail of death and misery. The thought of being a vessel for such malevolence terrified him, but not as much as the thought of dying.

Determined to save himself, Niran sought the help of a spirit doctor, a rare practitioner of ancient rituals capable of banishing malevolent spirits. The spirit doctor, an old and wise woman, performed a ritual that involved a spirit dancer—an ethereal figure whose movements could draw out the Phi Pop from its host.

As the ritual commenced, Niran watched in awe as the spirit dancer swayed gracefully, her movements mesmerizing and haunting. He felt the entity within him stir, resisting the call of the dancer's ethereal presence.

But the battle within Niran was far from over. The Phi Pop fought fiercely to maintain its hold, unwilling to release its grip on its new host. The dance intensified, the spirit dancer spinning with heightened energy, her movements becoming a blur.

Niran felt as if there were a thousand blades inside his body cutting him to pieces. He wanted it to stop, but he needed the ritual to go on or he would surely die.

In that moment of turmoil, Niran felt a surge of strength from within. The fear that

Phi Pop

had consumed him transformed into resolve. He fought back against the malevolence, mustering every ounce of willpower to expel the Phi Pop from his body.

As the spirit dancer's movements reached a crescendo, the Phi Pop could no longer resist the pull. With a final burst of energy, it tore itself away from Niran's insides, releasing him from its sinister grasp.

Exhausted and relieved, Niran collapsed, the ordeal having taken its toll on his body and mind. The spirit doctor, with her ancient knowledge, offered him healing remedies to strengthen his spirit, body, and mind.

In the aftermath of the harrowing ordeal, Niran emerged a changed man. He no longer sought solace in the dark corners of the city but found solace in the embrace of his loved ones.

YETI

THE LEGENDARY APELIKE CRYPTID OF THE HIMALAYAS

FREAKY FACTS

LOCATION: HIMALAYAS

FIRST SIGHTINGS: 1832

CLASSIFICATION: APELIKE

PERSONALITY: MYSTERIOUS, SHY, AND ELUSIVE

The legend of the Yeti has gained worldwide recognition, much like Bigfoot, appearing in films and animation. In the Western world, it is more commonly known as the Abominable Snowman.

Described as an apelike creature, the Yeti stands approximately 6 feet (2 m) tall and possesses a muscular build. Its body is covered in gray or reddish-brown fur, and it is large in size, weighing between 200 and 400 pounds (91 and 181 kg).

Believed to inhabit the mountainous regions of Asia, the Yeti is often thought to reside below the snow line of the Himalayas, where it frequently leaves tracks in the snow.

Many of the Himalayan folktales that refer to the Yeti as defenders of the mountains are cautionary tales. They portray the nefarious acts committed by these feared animals upon those who stray too far from home or who become lost in the vast icy expanses at night. They are sometimes attributed to guarding the gods who dwell in the Himalayas from bothersome, intruding humans.

According to legend, there are three types of Yetis. The largest is the Nyalmo, characterized by its black fur and formidable nature. Standing at around 15 feet (5 m) tall and resembling a bear, this man-eating Yeti primarily hunts yaks, snapping their necks by twisting their horns. There are rumors of their interactions with humans, including capturing and mating with them.

The next type is the Chuti, reaching a height of approximately 8 feet (2 m). They possess black fur, a short neck, and smaller feet compared to their hands. These omnivorous Yetis dwell at altitudes between 8,000 and 10,000 feet (2,438 and 3,048 m).

The last type is known as the Ban Jhakri or Rang Shin Bombo, meaning "forest shaman." While some literature does not classify them as Yetis, they are included in the legend. The Ban Jhakri is the shortest of the three, with very long golden or red fur. They inhabit forests at lower altitudes and are primarily vegetarian. However, there are occasional reports of them abducting children to initiate them into shamanism.

In 1960, Sir Edmund Hillary, the first person to summit Mount Everest, searched for evidence of the Yeti but was unable to find any conclusive proof. Nevertheless, there have been numerous reports of Yeti sightings or footprints in various areas of India, Nepal, and Bhutan.

If you go to the Himalayas, respect the people who have lived there for centuries, respect their culture, and respect their land, but above all, respect their legends. Don't mess with the Yeti!

Among the Sherpas, Tenzin was known as a fearless and skilled mountaineer, leading expeditions through treacherous terrains. His weathered face bore the marks of countless

ORANG PENDEK

Legends speak of a mysterious great ape residing in the untouched depths of Sumatra's forests, unknown to science. Referred to as the Orang Pendek, meaning "short person," this creature is believed to inhabit the remote regions of the island's interior. Its presence is often associated with Kerinci Seblat National Park, a vast reserve encompassing mountains and forests located in the southern part of Sumatra.

Numerous theories have been proposed to explain the nature of this enigmatic creature. Some contend that it is simply a larger species of gibbon, while others speculate that it possesses humanlike characteristics.

encounters with the unforgiving mountains, but there was one legend he had yet to face—the legendary Yeti.

One day, Tenzin received a message from a wealthy foreigner who sought the thrill of capturing the Yeti on camera. Intrigued by the challenge, and enticed by the promise of a substantial payment, Tenzin agreed to guide the expedition, even though he had doubts about the Yeti's existence.

Eight people made up their group: Tenzin, four foreigners as the man's crew, and three Sherpa tour guides. The expedition party traveled further into the Himalayas, where the air became colder and the surroundings more desolate. The Sherpa tour guides talked quietly to one another while carefully scanning the area. They warned the visitors of dangers hidden in the shadows.

Night fell, and the icy winds howled through the crevices of the cliffs. The wealthy foreigner, eager to capture the creature on film, set up camp in a secluded spot, far away from the watchful eyes of the Sherpas. Tenzin and the guides were uneasy, sensing an unsettling presence in the stillness of the night.

Despite the unease of the others, the foreigner insisted on setting up bait and traps around the camp to lure the Yeti. He was determined to capture the creature on film and make history with his discovery. The Sherpas tried to dissuade him, warning that chasing

a creature as dangerous as the Yeti could lead to disastrous consequences, but their pleas fell on deaf ears.

As the night wore on, the camp fell into an eerie silence. Tenzin's instincts screamed at him to abandon the foolish expedition and head back to safety, but he couldn't just leave the foreigner and his crew, as they were his responsibility.

Suddenly, a bone-chilling roar pierced the silence, shaking the ground beneath them. The Sherpas recognized the sound immediately—it was the unmistakable call of the Yeti.

"What have we done?" Tenzin muttered, regret gnawing at his heart.

The wealthy foreigner's eyes lit up with excitement as he grabbed his camera, oblivious to the danger that lurked in the darkness. "This is it! We're going to get it on film!" he exclaimed, rushing toward the source of the roar.

Tenzin, the man's crew, and the other Sherpa guides tried to stop him, but he was driven by his obsession. In his desperation to capture the elusive Yeti, he stumbled into a hidden crevice, disappearing from sight.

The rest of the group hurried to the spot, but it was too late. The wealthy foreigner had fallen into a deep ravine, and his lifeless body lay sprawled on the rocky floor.

Tenzin's heart sank, and guilt washed over him. The expedition had ended in tragedy, and he couldn't help but feel responsible for the man's death. His fears had been justified, and now a life had been lost in pursuit of a dangerous legend.

The group returned to their basecamp, somber and disheartened. The Sherpas mourned the loss of their companion, and Tenzin carried the weight of guilt on his shoulders. He had ignored his instincts, driven by the allure of money and adventure, and it had cost someone their life.

The tragic ending of the expedition served as a harsh reminder of the dangers of chasing mythical creatures and the importance of respecting the untamed wilderness. Tenzin vowed never to allow his curiosity or the temptation of money to blind him to the risks that lay ahead. He shared the story of the tragic expedition, reminding people that some legends are best left untouched.

And the Yeti remained in the mountains undisturbed and undiscovered, a mysterious guardian of the Himalayas.

MANANANGGAL

THE BODY-SPLITTING VISCERA SUCKER FROM THE PHILIPPINES

FREAKY FACTS

LOCATION: PHILIPPINES

FIRST SIGHTING: PREDATES WRITTEN HISTORY

CLASSIFICATION: VAMPIRE

PERSONALITY: BLOODTHIRSTY, CUNNING, PREDATOR, TERRIFYING, AND MALEVOLENT

There are numerous creatures in folklore that crave bloody human innards, but one of the most disturbing is the Manananggal from the Philippines.

In Filipino folklore, vampires, Ghouls (see page 152), viscera-suckers, and shapeshifters are all referred to as aswang. The Manananggal, which comes from the Tagalog word *tanggal*, meaning "to remove" or "to separate," is a viscera-sucking aswang.

KUNTILANAK

Known as the Kuntilanak in Indonesia and the Pontianak in Malay, this vampiric creature is believed to be created when a woman dies while pregnant or during childbirth. While she may initially appear as an attractive woman to lure her prey, her true form is hideous. She possesses black, empty sockets in place of her eyes, sharp claws, fangs, and sometimes even holes in the back of her neck.

The Kuntilanak resides in trees, patiently waiting for her next victim, often targeting children, whom she prefers. When she spots her prey, she emits a horrifying cry and swoops down, using her claws or fangs to tear them open and drink their blood.

A vampire-like creature, during the day the Manananggal appears as a beautiful young woman, but at night she transforms into something hideous and evil. Skilled at concealing her true form, she has friends and family and blends well within her community.

She preys on pregnant women, couples, and grooms, possibly because she was left at the altar or jilted by a lover and seeks revenge on anyone who has what she lost.

When night falls, the Manananggal grows bat-like wings, detaches her upper torso from her lower body, and takes flight in search of her next victim. As she soars through the moonlit sky, you may catch a glimpse of her intestines dangling from her split body.

Some say that the Manananggal may chant a spell while massaging a special lotion onto her body. This causes her eyes to grow wild and large, her hair to become matted, her teeth to become long fangs, and her fingers to change into long, jagged claws.

She preys on unsuspecting, sleeping victims, using her long red tubular tongue to reach through openings in windows or doors. She feeds on her victims through their mouth, nose, ears, or abdomen.

The Manananggal craves disgusting things like phlegm from sick individuals, as well as hearts, livers, lungs, and intestines. However, a living fetus is considered a delicacy to her, making pregnant women her favored prey.

Some claim that, on occasion, the Manananggal is accompanied by a small bird known as the tiktik, so-named for the sound it makes. The Manananggal is farther away when the tiktik is louder. If the bird is quiet, the Manananggal is nearby.

Placing pots of ash, salt, or uncooked rice around the house can help keep the Manananggal away from your home. It's possible that the Manananggal won't enter the house if she sees these items.

Happy couples are less likely to fall victim to the Manananggal. So be sure to treat your special someone with kindness and love, or you may just end up alone until the dreaded Manananggal makes you its next meal.

When a young married couple, Paul and Lyla, moved to Angeles City in the Philippines, their marriage was under strain. Lyla had been offered a huge promotion, and Paul gave up his career to follow her there. Paul, even though he had tried to be supportive, harbored a seed of resentment. As she worked long hours, his loneliness caused that seed to take root and grow.

He began to frequent a popular bar located in the city, but he only drank and listened to music—at least in the beginning.

One fateful night, Lyla came home from work early. She claimed to feel ill and rejected Paul's advances. Hurt and angry, Paul stormed out and headed to the bar. Once there, he sat at the bar and watched as many of the men would leave with attractive women on their arms. He had become familiar with some of the girls' faces, but there was one regular in particular that he was looking for. She was one of the most beautiful women he had ever seen.

He didn't have to find her; she found him. It was almost as if she sensed his need. She walked up, her motions so sensuous that her every movement felt like foreplay. She had on a long red dress, split all the way up to the top of her hips on both sides. The neckline plunged down past her navel, revealing more than the dress hid.

Paul bought her a drink and they talked for a bit. She laughed at Paul's jokes and he began to feel something in her presence that he had been missing, so when she asked him to come to her place, he hesitated, but only for a moment. She gently grabbed his hand, led him out of the bar, and down the street to a small apartment. He eagerly followed her inside and then to the bedroom without asking any questions.

FREAKY FOLKLORE

He pulled her close and began kissing her neck, while sliding his hands up her shoulders, where he gently slid the sleeves of her dress down until the top was hanging at her waist.

He stood back long enough to take in the sight of her naked torso and watched hungrily as she worked the dress past her hips and let it drop to the floor.

He stepped toward her again, but she reached out and put her palm on his chest, shoving him so hard that he landed on the mattress with a grunt.

He thought his eyes were playing tricks on him when she began twisting her body at the waist, until he heard the sound of tearing flesh. Her skin was stretching in an impossible way as she shifted her body further around.

Paul couldn't believe what he was seeing; this woman was bending and twisting, causing her body to tear in half. Had someone drugged his drinks?

He crawled backward on the mattress until his back was against the wall just beneath the only window in the tiny room. He watched in horror as she separated her torso from her lower body. She stuck her hands inside her body and pushed herself away from her lower half.

Paul almost gagged as he swallowed out of reflex. His eyes must have been playing tricks on him. He watched as this beautiful woman turned into a monster. She ripped her torso from her lower half and plopped down on the mattress. There, she continued to squirm as two large lumps formed on her back and began to protrude.

He heard the tearing sound of flesh again as the lumps burst, and two appendages stretched forth and reached out across the room. Wings! This thing had grown wings in mere seconds.

His horror only grew as a long snakelike tongue slithered out of her mouth and across his leg.

"You smell delectable," she hissed.

Paul found himself regretting every decision he had made up to this point. He wanted nothing more than to be back home, curled up in bed next to Lyla. But it was too late; he had let bitterness fuel this indiscretion that would now cost him his life.

JINN

BORN OF SMOKELESS FIRE AND A DUAL NATURE

FREAKY FACTS

LOCATION: EGYPT, IRAN, AND
TÜRKIYE

FIRST WRITTEN MENTION:
QURAN

CLASSIFICATION: SHAPESHIFTER

PERSONALITY: BENEVOLENT OR
MALEVOLENT, FREE-WILLED,
MYSTERIOUS, AND COMPLEX

From Arab folklore emerges a legendary creature known
by various names across the world. Jinn, or Djinn, as it was
historically spelled, are shapeshifting spirits composed of fire
and air that embody a smokeless fusion of flames, akin to energy.
Devoid of a fixed form, Jinn have the ability to assume any shape,
often favoring terrifying forms that instill fear in humans.

According to Islamic beliefs, Jinn inhabit a realm separate from our own. In Arabic, they are referred to as Jana, meaning "to conceal" or "to hide," which explains their invisibility and the reason why many have denied their existence. Quranic and Sunnah teachings assert that Jinn were created before humans and possess a fiery nature due to their composition. As a result, their relationship with humankind is founded on fire. Like all individuals, Jinn are expected to follow Islam and worship God. While Jinn can be Muslim or non-Muslim, the majority of non-Muslim Jinn are aligned with Satan's army, making them the most well-known type of Jinn.

Jinn have the ability to manifest in the form of deceased individuals, a phenomenon that also evokes fear in humans. In Islam, deceased individuals do not return to this world but move on to the next, making ghosts and spirits manifestations of Jinn, as they take on the appearance of the dead. Possessing the swiftness of light and the strength of forty to sixty men, Jinn possess almost godlike abilities. They can, for example, convert mass into energy and vice versa. However, despite their supernatural powers, they lack intellectual capabilities.

Residing in a parallel universe, Jinn have extended lifespans across thousands of years. While they can perceive our dimension, they remain invisible to the human eye. The Islamic world affirms the existence of Jinn through the Quran and Hadith, with the word "Jinn" mentioned twenty-nine times in the Quran and an entire chapter dedicated to the subject. Different types of Jinn exist, each possessing varying strengths and abilities.

During their honeymoon in Türkiye, Jade and Shayan picked up a few souvenirs, but little did they know that one of them held something sinister and deadly.

Jade and Shayan were newlyweds, filled with excitement and love as they embarked on their dream honeymoon to İzmir. The bustling streets and vibrant colors enchanted them as they explored the city's wonders hand in hand. Among the myriad shops and markets, they stumbled upon a small antique store tucked away in a narrow alley.

Intrigued by the display of unique and ancient artifacts, they stepped inside the dimly lit shop. An old shopkeeper with a long white beard and piercing eyes greeted them warmly. He seemed to know the stories behind every object in the store.

As Jade and Shayan browsed the collection, their eyes were drawn to an exquisite trinket box adorned with intricate carvings. The shopkeeper approached them with a smile and told them that it was a rare piece from ancient times. He spoke of its rumored powers and how it was said to have held a powerful Jinn, made captive long ago.

Both fascinated and amused by the tale, the couple decided to purchase the box as a unique memento of their trip. Little did they know that their impulsive decision would unleash a sinister force.

Back in their room that night, as Jade was examining the trinket box with awe, she pricked her finger on the corner of the lid as she opened it. A tiny drop of blood dripped onto the velvet lining of the trinket box. The spot of blood began to grow until it took the form of a scorpion that crawled right out of the box.

Jade gasped in horror as the tiny scorpion scuttled across the bedspread. Shayan rushed to her side, to see if she had been stung, but before they could react, the scorpion disappeared under the bed.

"Where did it go?" Jade asked, her heart racing with fear.

"I don't know," Shayan replied, searching under the bed with a sense of urgency.

Suddenly, they heard a faint buzzing sound coming from under the bed. They looked at each other with puzzled expressions, wondering what could be causing the strange noise. Jade jumped off the bed as it began to shake, and a cloud of smoke began to pour from beneath it and filled the room.

The smoke began to swirl and take shape, forming the figure of a tall, imposing man with a muscular physique and dark, smoldering eyes. Jade and Shayan took a step back in fear as the man emerged from the smoke, towering over them. He was dressed in ancient clothing and had a sharp, regal look about him.

"I am the Jinn of the trinket box," he announced with a deep, commanding voice. "You have summoned me, and now I am bound to serve you."

Jade and Shayan stood frozen, staring at the Jinn in disbelief. They had heard stories about the power of the Jinn but never thought they would encounter one themselves. They exchanged a quick glance before Jade spoke, "Serve us? How?"

The Jinn chuckled. "Anything you desire, I can make it come true. I am bound to fulfill your wishes. However, be warned: Every wish comes with a price. You must choose wisely." His voice echoed like thunder in the room, making Jade and Shayan tremble with fear.

They looked at each other, unsure of what to do. The idea of having all their wishes granted was tempting, but they didn't know how high the price they would have to pay would be.

Jade whispered to Shayan, and he nodded his head. She then turned and spoke to the Jinn. "We want what no one ever wishes for in this situation. We want you to be free."

The Djinn's eyes widened in surprise. "You wish for my freedom?" he repeated incredulously. "No one has ever wished for that before."

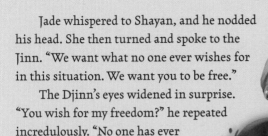

Jade and Shayan nodded in unison, determined to do the right thing. The Jinn smiled, a glimmer of gratitude in his eyes. "Very well," he said. "I am free."

With those words, the Jinn vanished into thin air, leaving behind only the trinket box. Jade and Shayan breathed a sigh of relief, happy to have made the right choice. They knew that they would never forget their encounter with the powerful Jinn.

As they settled back into bed, Jade realized something.

"Wait a minute," she said, "what about the price for our wish?"

Shayan looked at her with concern. "What do you mean?"

"Well," Jade said, "the Jinn said that every wish comes with a price. What's the price?"

Suddenly, the room began to shake violently, and the windows rattled in their frames. Jade and Shayan clung to each other, their hearts pounding with fear. The trinket box began to glow with an eerie light, and a voice boomed from within.

"The price for your wish is your souls!" the voice thundered. "You will be bound to me for all eternity, serving me in the afterlife!"

Jinn

CONCLUSION

In the eerie darkness that shrouds our world, we have explored the depths of human imagination, unveiling the chilling tales of the most terrifying cryptids, beasts, and monsters that haunt every corner of our vast continents. As we reach the final pages of this sinister collection, we find ourselves standing on the precipice of an unfathomable truth—that in the shadows of reality, the line between myth and actuality becomes blurred.

Throughout these chilling accounts, we have journeyed to the darkest corners of each continent, encountering creatures both grotesque and awe-inspiring. From the legendary Yeti roaming the snow-capped peaks of the Himalayas to the skin-crawling Chupacabra stalking the Americas, and from the enigmatic Mothman soaring over the forests of North America to the otherworldly Bunyip lurking in the Australian marshlands, each tale weaves a tapestry of fear and fascination, reminding us of the enduring power of folklore and the eternal human quest to explain the unexplained.

Beyond the realm of pure imagination, these accounts reveal glimpses of ancient ecosystems, untamed wildernesses, and the unknown depths of our collective subconscious. As our global cultures intermingle, these myths and legends have merged, adapting and evolving with each retelling, reminding us of the interconnectedness of all humanity and the shared universal fear of the unknown.

Yet among these terrifying beings there is also an invitation to ponder the profound and the peculiar, to embrace the mysteries that lie just beyond our understanding. For it is in these dark realms of myth that we confront our deepest fears, questioning the limits of our knowledge and the boundaries of our existence.

As we wrap up this eerie book, let us carry these spine-tingling tales with us, not as mere bedtime stories but as windows into the enigma that is life itself. For the world is far more than we can ever grasp, and the terrifying cryptids, beasts, and monsters that populate our folklore are mirrors reflecting the hidden depths of our collective soul.

In the end, perhaps it is in the embrace of the unknown that we find a spark of humility and curiosity, for in the vastness of our planet lies an infinite array of enigmas waiting to be uncovered. And as long as there are shadows to cast doubt upon the certainties of the day, the legends of these creatures will continue to whisper in our ears, reminding us that the world is an awe-inspiring and mysterious place, where every corner still holds secrets that can freeze the blood and quicken the pulse.

ACKNOWLEDGMENTS

As I stand at the end of this enthralling journey through the realm of folklore creatures, I am humbled and deeply grateful for the unwavering support and love of numerous individuals who made this book a reality. Their encouragement and belief in my passion for these mythical beings have propelled me forward, and for that I extend my heartfelt appreciation:

To my parents, who have been my pillars of strength and belief from the very beginning. Your unwavering encouragement and belief in my abilities have been the fuel that kept me going.

To my beloved children, you are the heartbeat of my existence. Your presence in my life gives me purpose and fills my heart with boundless love and inspiration. Your unwavering faith in me has been a driving force behind this endeavor.

To my mother-in-law, Debbie, who exuded genuine excitement and enthusiasm for my writing journey. Though you left us too soon, your memory continues to motivate me. I wish you could have held this book in your hands, as promised.

To my loving husband, who stood by my side through countless late nights and exhausting work hours. Your unwavering support, patience, and belief in my dreams have been my rock, and I am endlessly grateful.

To all of my podcast fans, your unwavering enthusiasm and engagement have inspired me every step of the way. Your feedback and support have been invaluable, and I am honored to have you on this journey with me.

Special thanks to Amy at Quarto, for taking a chance on me and giving me the opportunity to share my passion with the world. Your belief in my work has been a tremendous blessing.

Last but not least, to Darkness Prevails, who played a pivotal role in making this dream a reality. Your support, encouragement, and unwavering belief in me and my abilities have been the driving force behind this accomplishment. Without you, none of this would have ever been possible.

In writing this book, I have discovered the magic of storytelling and the allure of folklore creatures that have fascinated humanity for generations. It is with immense gratitude that I acknowledge the invaluable contributions of each person mentioned here and all those whose names remain unspoken but whose presence has shaped me as an author and as a person.

To all those whose names are mentioned and those who remain unnamed but have touched my life in ways I could never fully express, thank you. Your love, encouragement, and belief in me have been instrumental in bringing this book to fruition.

To all of you, I extend my deepest thanks and love. This book is a testament to the power of belief, passion, and the profound connection we share through folklore creatures, no matter how distant the origins or how diverse our backgrounds.

ABOUT THE AUTHOR

Carman Carrion is a name synonymous with the eerie and mysterious realms of folklore and horror. As the esteemed writer and host of the popular podcasts *Freaky Folklore* and *Destination Terror*, Carman has spent a lifetime immersed in the spine-tingling tales that have captured the human imagination for generations. Working as a dedicated contributor to the Eeriecast Podcast Network, Carman's dulcet voice and captivating storytelling have brought chilling narratives to life for countless listeners.

Carman Carrion finds inspiration in the serene beauty of the Ozarks region where she resides, balancing a love for the outdoors with a passion for the macabre. Carman's diverse interests include drawing, writing, and reading, often delving into the darkest corners of literature and art. An avid traveler, she seeks out mysterious locales that fuel her fascination with the unknown.

Yet, despite her deep connection to the realms of darkness, Carman also cherishes moments of joy and togetherness with her family, finding comfort in the embrace of loved ones. In essence, Carman Carrion embodies the perfect blend of a lifelong passion for the strange and an appreciation for the simple pleasures of life.

REFERENCES

A Book of Creatures (blog). https://abookofcreatures.com/.

Alexander, Kathy. *Legends of America* (blog). https://www.legendsofamerica.com/.

Atsma, Aaron J., ed. Theoi Project—Greek Mythology. https://www.theoi.com/.

Blackman, W. Haden. *The Field Guide to North American Monsters*. New York: Three Rivers Press, 1998.

Egerkrans, Johan, trans. Susan Beard. *Vaesen: Spirits and Monsters of Scandinavian Folklore*. Stockholm: B Wahlströms, 2013.

Encyclopedia Mythica. https://pantheon.org/.

Hellberg, Niklas. *Encyclopedia Mythologica*. https://encyclopediamythologica.com/home.

Krensky, Stephen. *The Book of Mythical Beasts and Magical Creatures*. New York: Penguin Random House, 2020.

LoreThrill: Fables and Legends. https://lorethrill.com/.

McElroy, D.R. *Superstitions: A Handbook of Folklore, Myths, and Legends from Around the World*. New York: Quarto, 2020.

Meyer, Matthew. Yokai.com. https://yokai.com/.

Navarro, Hector and E.L. Soto. *Myths, Mysteries & Monsters* (podcast), part of Factschology. https://factschology.com/.

Shepard, Tracy. *The Compendium of Arcane Beasts and Critters* (blog). https://arcanebeastsandcritters.wordpress.com/.

Sky History. AETN UK. https://www.history.co.uk/.

Stone, Zayden. *Mythical Creaturwes and Magical Beasts: Volume 2*. Spent Pens Publications, 2022.

University of Southern California (USC) Digital Folklore Archives. https://folklore.usc.edu/.

REFERENCES

—

CREATURE KEY

AMERICAS

SKINWALKER 10   BIGFOOT 15   BEAST OF BRAY ROAD 20   GOATMAN 24

WENDIGO 28   JERSEY DEVIL 33   MOTHMAN 38

FREAKY FOLKLORE

MICHIGAN DOGMAN 42

WAHEELA 47

KUSHTAKA 52

LA LLORONA 56

PISHTACO 60

CHUPACABRA 63

EL SOMBRERÓN 66

DUENDE 70

EL CULEBRÓN 74

CREATURE KEY

EUROPE

BANSHEE 80

MYLING 84

VODYANOY 88

WEREWOLF 92

KELPIE 96

BLACK SHUCK 100

FREAKY FOLKLORE

246

NUCKELAVEE 104

OGRE 108

BABA YAGA 112

STRZYGA 116

EL CUCUY 120

CREATURE KEY

—

247

AFRICA

TOKOLOS-
HE 126

ADZE 130

BULTUNGIN
(WEREHYE-
NA) 134

KAMAPPA 139

IMPUNDULU 144

GROOT-
SLANG 148

GHOUL 152

AUSTRALIA AND NEW ZEALAND

YARA-MA-YHA-
WHO 158

BUNYIP 162

BURRUNJOR 167

YOWIE 172

DROP
BEAR 176

MOEHAU 183

MULDJEWANGK 188

CREATURE KEY

ASIA

YUKI-ONNA 194

JIANGSHI 199

SHUTEN-DOJI 204

KRASUE 208

HACHISHAKUSAMA 212

KUCHISAKE-ON-
NA 216

PHI POP 220

YETI 224

MANANANGGAL 229

JINN 234

CREATURE KEY

—

INDEX

INDEX

© 2024 by Quarto Publishing Group USA Inc.
Text © 2024 by Darkness Prevails

First published in 2024 by Wellfleet Press,
an imprint of The Quarto Group,
142 West 36th Street, 4th Floor,
New York, NY 10018, USA
(212) 779-4972
www.Quarto.com

Wellfleet Press titles are also available at discount for retail, wholesale, promotional, and bulk purchase.
For details, contact the Special Sales Manager by email at specialsales@quarto.com or by mail at The
Quarto Group, Attn: Special Sales Manager, 100 Cummings Center Suite 265D, Beverly, MA 01915 USA.

10 9 8 7 6 5 4 3

ISBN: 978-1-57715-441-9

Digital edition published in 2024
eISBN: 978-0-7603-8990-4

Library of Congress Control Number: 2023951662

Group Publisher: Rage Kindelsperger
Editorial Director: Erin Canning
Creative Director: Laura Drew
Managing Editor: Cara Donaldson
Editor: Elizabeth You
Cover Design: Scott Richardson
Interior Design: Annie Marino
Cover Illustration: Jen Santos
Interior Illustrations: Gunship Revolution's Jen Santos, Marcus Reyno, Timothy Terrenal,
and Mara Miranda-Escota

Printed in China